## Contents

# foreword

This handbook is designed for Federal supervisors and employees and presents an eight-step process for developing employee performance plans that are aligned with and support organizational goals. It also provides guidelines for writing performance elements and standards that not only meet regulatory requirements, but also maximize the capability that performance plans have for focusing employee efforts on achieving organizational and group goals.

The methods presented here are designed to develop elements and standards that measure employee and work unit accomplishments rather than to develop other measures that are often used in appraising performance, such as measuring behaviors or competencies. Although this handbook includes a discussion of the importance of balancing measures, the main focus presented here is to measure accomplishments. Consequently, much of the information presented in the first five steps of this eight-step process applies when supervisors and employees want to measure results. However, the material presented in Steps 6 through 8 about developing standards, monitoring performance, and checking the performance plan apply to all measurement approaches.

# foreword

The handbook has four chapters and three appendices:

- CHAPTER 1 gives the background and context of performance management that you will need to understand before beginning the eight-step process.

- CHAPTER 2 defines **accomplishments,** which is key to using this handbook successfully.

- CHAPTER 3 includes a detailed description of the **eight-step process** for developing employee performance plans that are aligned with and support organizational goals.

- CHAPTER 4 provides **study tools**, including a followup **quiz** and a **quick reference** for the eight-step process.

- THE APPENDICES contain **example standards** that were written specifically for **appraisal programs** that appraise performance on elements at five, three, and two levels.

After reading the instructional material, studying the examples, and completing the exercises in this book, you should be able to:

- DEVELOP a performance plan that aligns individual performance with organizational goals

- USE a variety of methods to determine work unit and individual accomplishments

- DETERMINE the difference between activities and accomplishments

- EXPLAIN regulatory requirements for employee performance plans

Remember the story about the naive student in his first English literature course who was worried because he didn't know what prose was? When he found out that prose was ordinary speech, he exclaimed, "Wow! I've been speaking prose all my life!"

Managing performance well is like speaking prose. Many managers have been "speaking" and practicing effective performance management naturally all their supervisory lives, but don't know it!

Some people mistakenly assume that performance management is concerned only with following regulatory requirements to appraise and rate performance. Actually, assigning ratings of record is only **one part** of the overall process (and perhaps the least important part).

Performance management is the systematic process of:

- **planning** work and setting expectations

- continually **monitoring** performance

- **developing** the capacity to perform

- periodically **rating** performance in a summary fashion

- **rewarding** good performance

The revisions made in 1995 to the governmentwide performance appraisal and awards regulations support "natural" performance management. Great care was taken to ensure that the requirements those regulations establish would complement and not conflict with the kinds of activities and actions effective managers are practicing as a matter of course.

**PLANNING** In an effective organization, work is planned out in advance. Planning means setting performance expectations and goals for groups and individuals to channel their efforts toward achieving organizational objectives. Getting employees involved in the planning process will help them understand the goals of the organization, what needs to be done, why it needs to be done, and how well it should be done.

The regulatory requirements for planning employees' performance include establishing the elements and standards of their performance appraisal plans. Performance elements and standards should be measurable, understandable, verifiable, equitable, and achievable. Through critical elements, employees are held accountable as individuals for work assignments or responsibilities. Employee performance plans should be flexible so that they can be adjusted for changing program objectives and work requirements. When used effectively, these plans can be beneficial working documents that are discussed often, and not merely paper work that is filed in a drawer and seen only when ratings of record are required.

**MONITORING** In an effective organization, assignments and projects are monitored continually. Monitoring well means consistently measuring performance and providing ongoing feedback to employees and work groups on their progress toward reaching their goals.

The regulatory requirements for monitoring performance include conducting progress reviews with employees where their performance is compared against their elements and standards. Ongoing monitoring provides the supervisor the opportunity to check how well employees are meeting predetermined standards and to make changes to unrealistic or problematic standards. By monitoring continually, supervisors can identify unacceptable performance at any time during the appraisal period and provide assistance to address such performance rather than wait until the end of the period when summary rating levels are assigned.

PERFORMANCE MANAGEMENT'S FIVE KEY COMPONENTS

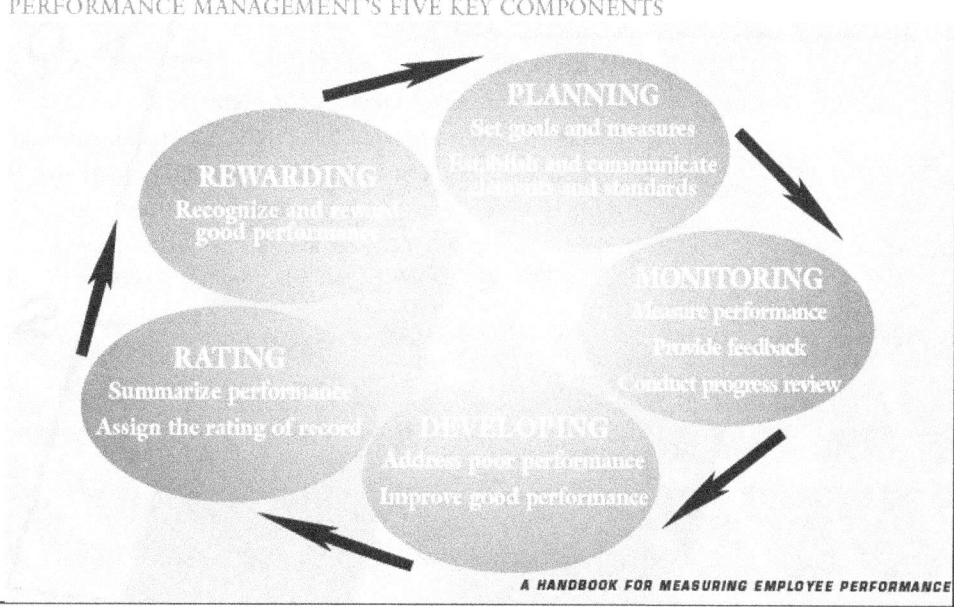

DEVELOPING  In an effective organization, employee developmental needs are evaluated and addressed. Developing in this instance means increasing the capacity to perform through training, giving assignments that introduce new skills or higher levels of responsibility, improving work processes, or other methods. Providing employees with training and developmental opportunities encourages good performance, strengthens job-related skills and competencies, and helps employees keep up with changes in the workplace, such as the introduction of new technology .

Carrying out the processes of performance management provides an excellent opportunity for supervisors and employees to identify developmental needs. While planning and monitoring work, deficiencies in performance become evident and should be addressed. Areas for improving good performance also stand out, and action can be taken to help successful employees improve even further.

RATING  From time to time, organizations find it useful to summarize employee performance. This helps with comparing performance over time or across a set of employees. Organizations need to know who their best performers are.

Within the context of formal performance appraisal requirements, rating means evaluating employee or group performance against the elements and standards in an employee's performance plan and assigning a summary rating of record. The rating of record is assigned according to procedures included in the organization's appraisal program. It is based on work performed during an entire appraisal period. The rating of record has a bearing on various other personnel actions, such as granting within-grade pay increases and determining additional retention service credit in a reduction in force.

REWARDING  In an effective organization, rewards are used often and well. Rewarding means recognizing employees, individually and as members of groups, for their performance and acknowledging their contributions to the agency's mission. A basic principle of effective management is that all behavior is controlled by its consequences. Those consequences can and should be both formal and informal and both positive and negative.

Good managers don't wait for their organization to solicit nominations for formal awards before recognizing good performance. Recognition is an ongoing, natural part of day-to-day experience. A lot of the actions that reward good performance, like saying "thank you," don't require a specific regulatory authority. Nonetheless, awards regulations provide a broad range of forms that more formal rewards can take, such as cash, time off, and many recognition items. The regulations also cover a variety of contributions that can be rewarded, from suggestions to group accomplishments.

PERFORMANCE MANAGEMENT AS PROSE

Good managers have been speaking and practicing effective performance management all their lives, executing each key component process well. They not only set goals and plan work routinely, but they also measure progress toward those goals and give feedback to employees. They set high standards, but they also take care to develop the skills needed to reach them. They also use formal and informal rewards to recognize the behavior and results that accomplish their mission. All five components working together and supporting each other achieve natural, effective performance management.

# Employee Performance Plans

Employees must know what they need to do to perform their jobs successfully. Expectations for employee performance are established in employee performance plans. Employee performance plans are all of the written, or otherwise recorded, performance elements that set forth expected performance. A plan must include all critical and non-critical elements and their performance standards.

Performance elements tell employees **what** they have to do and standards tell them **how well** they have to do it. Developing elements and standards that are understandable, measurable, attainable, fair, and challenging is vital to the effectiveness of the performance appraisal process and is what this handbook is all about.

Federal regulations define three types of elements: critical elements, non-critical elements, and additional performance elements. Agency appraisal programs are required to use critical elements (although the agency may choose to call them something else), but the other two types can be used at the agency's option. Before continuing further with this handbook, you should contact your human resources office to determine the types of elements your appraisal program allows.

## A NOTE ABOUT PERFORMANCE PLANS

*This handbook is about developing employee performance plans. However, there is another type of performance plan that you need to be aware of. The Government Performance and Results Act of 1993 requires each agency to prepare an annual performance plan covering each program activity set forth in its budget. These organizational performance plans:*

- *establish program-level performance goals that are objective, quantifiable, and measurable*
- *describe the operational resources needed to meet those goals*
- *establish performance indicators to be used in measuring the outcomes of each program*

*We will be using organizational performance plans during Step 1 of the eight-step process presented in this handbook. Organizational performance plans are key in the process of aligning employee performance with organizational goals.*

## A NOTE ABOUT GROUP OR TEAM PERFORMANCE

*The term "group or team performance" can be confusing sometimes. When we say that critical elements cannot describe group performance, we are saying that the group's performance as a whole cannot be used as a critical element. This does not preclude describing an individual's contribution to the group as a critical element. The key to distinguishing between group performance and an individual's contribution to the group is that group performance is measured at an aggregate level, not for a single employee. An individual's contribution to the group is measured at the individual employee level.*

CRITICAL ELEMENTS  A critical element is an assignment or responsibility of such importance that unacceptable performance in that element would result in a determination that the employee's overall performance is unacceptable. Regulations require that each employee have at least one critical element in his or her performance plan. Even though no maximum number is placed on the number of critical elements possible, most experts in the field of performance management agree that between three and seven critical elements are appropriate for most work situations.

Critical elements are the cornerstone of individual accountability in employee performance management. Unacceptable performance is defined in Section 4301(3) of title 5, United States Code, as failure on one or more critical elements, which can result in the employee's reassignment, removal, or reduction in grade. Consequently, critical elements must describe work assignments and responsibilities that are within the employee's control. For most employees this means that critical elements **cannot** describe a group's performance.  However, a supervisor or manager can and should be held accountable for seeing that results measured at the group or team level are achieved. Critical elements assessing group performance may be appropriate to include in the performance plan of a supervisor, manager, or team leader who can reasonably be expected to command the production and resources necessary to achieve the results (i.e., be held individually accountable).

**NON-CRITICAL ELEMENTS**  A non-critical element is a dimension or aspect of individual, team, or organizational performance, exclusive of a critical element, that is used in assigning a summary level. Important aspects of non-critical elements include:

NO PERFORMANCE-BASED ACTIONS  Failure on a non-critical element **cannot** be used as the basis for a performance-based adverse action, such as a demotion or removal. Only critical elements may be used that way. Moreover, if an employee fails on a non-critical element, the employee's performance cannot be summarized as *Unacceptable* overall based on that failure.

GROUP PERFORMANCE  Non-critical elements are the only way an agency can include the group's or the team's performance as an element in the performance plan so that it counts in the summary level. For example, team structured organizations might use a non-critical element to plan, track, and appraise the team on achieving its goals. To do this, each team member's performance plan would include the "team" element (i.e., a non-critical element) and the rating for the team on that element would be counted in the summary level of each team member.

WHEN THEY CAN'T BE USED  Non-critical elements cannot be used in appraisal programs that use only two levels to summarize performance in the rating of record. This is because they would have no effect on the summary rating level and, by definition, they must affect the summary level. (That is, in a two-level program, failure on non-critical elements cannot bring the summary level down to *Unacceptable,* and assessments of non-critical elements cannot raise the summary level to *Fully Successful* if a critical element is failed.)

CAN GREATLY AFFECT THE SUMMARY LEVEL  Sometimes the word "non-critical" is interpreted to mean "not as important." Prior to 1995, this interpretation was prescribed by regulation. Now, however, depending on how an appraisal program is designed, this need not be the case. Even though consideration of non-critical elements cannot result in assigning an *Unacceptable* summary level, appraisal programs can be designed so that non-critical elements have as much weight or more weight than critical elements in determining summary levels above *Unacceptable*.

**BEFORE YOU CAN USE NON-CRITICAL ELEMENTS IN EMPLOYEE PERFORMANCE PLANS, YOU MUST DETERMINE IF YOUR APPRAISAL PROGRAM ALLOWS THEM.**

## ADDITIONAL PERFORMANCE ELEMENTS

An additional performance element is a dimension or aspect of individual, team, or organizational performance that is not a critical element and is not used in assigning a summary rating level. The essential difference between a non-critical element and an additional performance element is that non-critical elements **do** affect the summary level. Otherwise, the features and limitations of non-critical elements discussed above also apply to additional performance elements. Opportunities for using additional performance elements include:

**CHECK THE RULES OF YOUR PROGRAM BEFORE INCLUDING ADDITIONAL PERFORMANCE ELEMENTS IN YOUR PLANS.**

| NEW WORK ASSIGNMENT  Managers and employees may want to establish goals, track and measure performance, and develop skills for an aspect of work that they do not believe should count in the summary level. For example, if an employee volunteered to work on a new project that requires new skills, an additional performance element describing the new assignment provides a non-threatening vehicle for planning, measuring, and giving feedback on the employee's performance without counting it in the summary level.

| GROUP PERFORMANCE  In a two-level appraisal program, additional performance elements are the only way to include a discussion of group performance in the appraisal process. Even though the element assessment does not count when determining the summary level, managers and employees could use it to manage the group's performance.

| AWARDS   Additional performance elements can be used to establish criteria for determining awards eligibility, especially in a two-level program that no longer bases awards solely on a summary level.

## ELEMENT CHARACTERISTICS

| | REQUIRED IN EMPLOYEE PERFORMANCE PLANS | CREDITED IN THE SUMMARY LEVEL | CAN DESCRIBE A GROUP'S PERFORMANCE |
|---|---|---|---|
| CRITICAL ELEMENTS | YES | YES | NO* |
| NON-CRITICAL ELEMENTS | NO | YES | YES |
| ADDITIONAL PERFORMANCE ELEMENTS | NO | NO | YES |

*Except when written for a supervisor or manager who has individual management control over a group's production and resources.

Additional performance elements were introduced in the September 1995 performance appraisal regulations and have not been used widely yet. We foresee their popularity rising as agencies discover the possibilities they present for managing performance.

## KNOW YOUR PROGRAM FEATURES

Again, it is important to stress that before you continue with this handbook, you need to find out the rules established by your appraisal program; specifically, you will need to know:

- which kinds of elements your program allows you to use

- at how many levels your program appraises employee performance on elements

- how many summary levels your program uses

- if your program allows weighting of elements (see Step 4)

- whether the program requires specific elements and/or uses generic standards

## example program features

This handbook uses an example agency called the "Federal Benefits Bureau," (FBB) which is an agency that specializes in benefits and retirement services. To be able to understand and work through the examples, you need to know the features of FBB's appraisal program (i.e., the same features listed above).
FBB's appraisal program:

- uses critical, non-critical, and additional performance elements

- appraises employee performance on elements at five levels:

    *Unacceptable*
    *Minimally Successful*
    *Fully Successful*
    *Exceeds Fully Successful*
    *Outstanding*

- uses five summary levels, which are the same as the elements' five levels listed above

- allows elements to be weighted according to importance to the organization

- requires **no** specific or generic elements

# chapter 2

## DISTINGUISHING ACTIVITIES FROM ACCOMPLISHMENTS

*CHAPTER 2 DISCUSSES WHAT MAY BE THE MOST IMPORTANT CONCEPT IN THIS HANDBOOK: THE DIFFERENCE BETWEEN MEASURING ACTIVITIES AND MEASURING ACCOMPLISHMENTS. THE FOLLOWING STORY ILLUSTRATES THIS CONCEPT.*

# The Beekeepers and Their Bees

Once upon a time, there were two beekeepers who each had a beehive. The beekeepers worked for a company called Bees, Inc. The company's customers loved its honey and wanted the business to produce more honey than it had the previous year. As a result, each beekeeper was told to produce more honey at the same quality. With different ideas about how to do this, the beekeepers designed different approaches to improve the performance of their hives.

The first beekeeper established a bee performance management approach that measured how many flowers each bee visited. At considerable cost to the beekeeper, an extensive measurement system was created to count the flowers each bee visited. The beekeeper provided feedback to each bee at midseason on his individual performance, but the bees were never told about the hive's goal to produce more honey so that Bees, Inc., could increase honey sales. The beekeeper created special awards for the bees who visited the most flowers.

The second beekeeper also established a bee performance management approach, but this approach communicated to each bee the goal of the hive—to produce more honey. This beekeeper and his bees measured two aspects of their performance: the amount of nectar each bee brought back to the hive and the amount of honey the hive produced. The performance of each bee and the hive's overall performance were charted and posted on the hive's bulletin board for all bees to see. The beekeeper created a few awards for the bees that gathered the most nectar, but he also established a hive incentive program that rewarded each bee in the hive based on the hive's production of honey—the more honey produced the more recognition each bee would receive.

# chapter 2

At the end of the season, the beekeepers evaluated their approaches. The first beekeeper found that his hive had indeed increased the number of flowers visited, but the amount of honey produced by the hive had dropped. The Queen Bee reported that because the bees were so busy trying to visit as many flowers as possible, they limited the amount of nectar they would carry so they could fly faster. Also, because the bees felt they were competing against each other for awards (because only the top performers were recognized), they would not share valuable information with each other (like the location of the flower-filled fields they'd spotted on the way back to the hive) that could have helped improve the performance of all the bees. (After all was said and done, one of the high-performing bees told the beekeeper that if he'd been told that the real goal was to make more honey rather than to visit more flowers, he would have done his work completely differently.) As the beekeeper handed out the awards to individual bees, unhappy buzzing was heard in the background.

The second beekeeper, however, had very different results. Because each bee in his hive was focused on the hive's goal of producing more honey, the bees had concentrated their efforts on gathering more nectar to produce more honey than ever before. The bees worked together to determine the highest nectar-yielding flowers and to create quicker processes for depositing the nectar they'd gathered. They also worked together to help increase the amount of nectar gathered by the poor performers. The Queen Bee of this hive reported that the poor performers either improved their performance or transferred to another hive. Because the hive had reached its goal, the beekeeper awarded each bee his portion of the hive incentive payment. The beekeeper was also surprised to hear a loud, happy buzz and a jubilant flapping of wings as he rewarded the individual high-performing bees with special recognition.

THE MORAL OF THIS STORY IS:  MEASURING AND RECOGNIZING ACCOMPLISHMENTS RATHER THAN ACTIVITIES—AND GIVING FEEDBACK TO THE WORKER BEES—OFTEN IMPROVES THE RESULTS OF THE HIVE.

Although it somewhat oversimplifies performance management, the beekeepers' story illustrates the importance of measuring and recognizing accomplishments (the amount of honey production per hive) rather than activities (visiting flowers). This handbook is designed to help you develop elements and standards that center around accomplishments, not activities.

The chart below depicts the type of measurement that should occur at each organizational level of Bees, Inc., and includes measurements used by the beekeepers.

**PERFORMANCE PYRAMID**
*Note that outputs occur at two levels—the work unit and the employee level.*

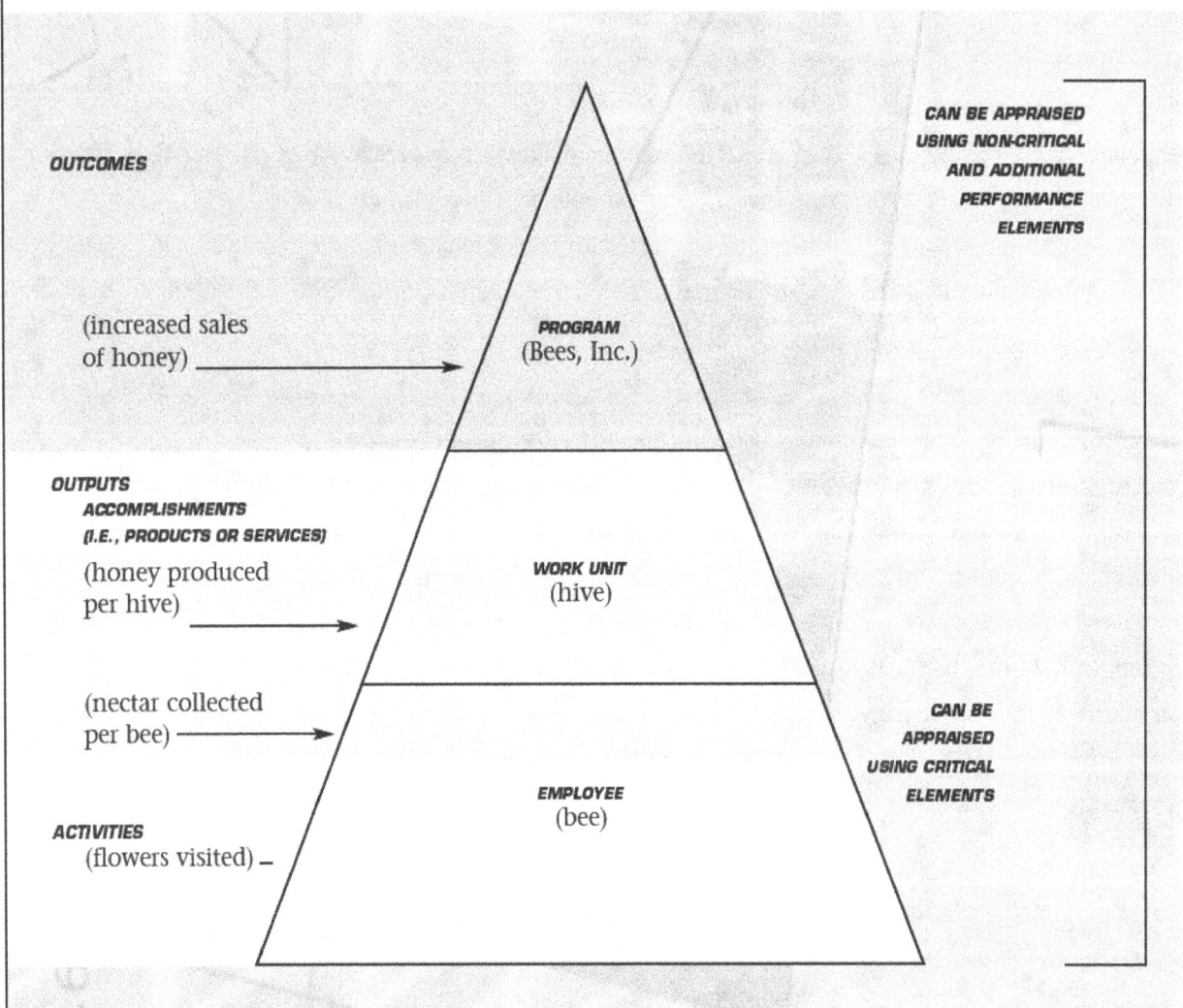

OUTCOMES

(increased sales of honey) ⟶ **PROGRAM** (Bees, Inc.)

OUTPUTS
ACCOMPLISHMENTS
(I.E., PRODUCTS OR SERVICES)

(honey produced per hive) ⟶ **WORK UNIT** (hive)

(nectar collected per bee) ⟶ **EMPLOYEE** (bee)

ACTIVITIES
(flowers visited)

CAN BE APPRAISED USING NON-CRITICAL AND ADDITIONAL PERFORMANCE ELEMENTS

CAN BE APPRAISED USING CRITICAL ELEMENTS

**Activities** are the actions taken to produce results and are generally described using verbs. In the beekeeper story, the *activity* being measured was *visiting* flowers. Other examples of activities include:

- *filing* documents
- *developing* software programs
- *answering* customer questions
- *writing* reports

**Accomplishments** (or outputs) are the products or services (the results) of employee and work unit activities and are generally described using nouns. The examples of *outputs* used in the story include the amount of *nectar* each bee collected and the *honey* production for the hive. Other examples include:

- *files* that are orderly and complete
- a software *program* that works
- accurate *guidance* to customers
- a *report* that is complete and accurate

**Outcomes** are the final results of an agency's products and services (and other outside factors that may affect performance). The example of an outcome used in the beekeeper story was increased sales of honey for Bees, Inc. Other examples of outcomes could include:

- reduced number of transportation-related deaths
- improved fish hatcheries
- a decrease in the rate of teenage alcoholism
- clean air

*Because of the requirements set by the Government Performance and Results Act of 1993 (i.e., the Results Act), Federal agencies are measuring their organizational outcomes and outputs. The Results Act requires agencies to have strategic plans, which include outcome-related goals and objectives for the major functions and operations of the agency. Those outcome goals must be objective, quantifiable, and measurable. The Results Act also requires agencies to develop annual performance plans that cover each one of their programs. Performance plans must include performance goals, which define the annual, often incremental, progress in achieving the outcome goals in the strategic plan. Performance goals are often output-oriented because they address single-year performance. We will talk more about strategic plans with their outcome goals, and performance plans with their output goals, in Chapter 3.*

On the performance pyramid illustrated on page 14, notice that accomplishments can be measured at two levels in the organization—the employee level and the work unit level. Employee accomplishments can be included in employee performance plans using all three types of performance elements. Work unit accomplishments also can be included in the appraisal process—through non-critical elements if the agency desires to have work unit performance affect ratings (and only if the appraisal program uses more than two summary levels) or through additional performance elements if work unit performance is not to affect ratings. However they are used in performance appraisal, work unit as well as employee accomplishments can always be recognized through an awards program.

If supervisors, team leaders, and employees want to develop performance plans that support the achievement of organizational outcomes, they might try the second beekeeper's approach of sharing organizational goals with the hive, measuring and rewarding accomplishments rather than activities, and providing feedback on performance.

# Using Balanced Measures

*THIS HANDBOOK FOCUSES ON MEASURING ACCOMPLISHMENTS AT THE WORK UNIT AND EMPLOYEE LEVELS. THERE MAY BE SITUATIONS, HOWEVER, WHEN ACTIVITIES, BEHAVIORS, OR PROCESSES MAY BE IMPORTANT TO INCLUDE IN AN EMPLOYEE'S PERFORMANCE PLAN. THIS HANDBOOK DOES NOT FOCUS ON HOW TO DEVELOP THOSE KINDS OF MEASURES. HOWEVER, WE WOULD BE REMISS NOT TO INCLUDE A DISCUSSION ABOUT THE IMPORTANCE OF BALANCING MEASURES IN YOUR MEASUREMENT SYSTEM. THEREFORE, A SHORT DESCRIPTION OF BALANCED MEASURES FOLLOWS.*

Traditionally, many agencies have measured their organizational performance by focusing on internal or process performance, looking at factors such as the number of full-time equivalents (FTEs) allotted, the number of programs controlled by the agency, or the size of the budget for the fiscal year. In contrast, private sector businesses usually focus on the financial measures of their bottom line: return-on-investment, market share, and earnings-per-share. Alone, neither of these approaches provides the full perspective on an organization's performance that a manager needs to manage effectively. But by balancing customer and employee satisfaction measures with results and financial measures, managers will have a more complete picture and will know where to make improvements.

BALANCING MEASURES Robert S. Kaplan and David P. Norton have developed a set of measures that they refer to as "a balanced scorecard." These measures give top managers a fast but comprehensive view of the organization's performance and include both process and results measures. Kaplan and Norton compare the balanced scorecard to the dials and indicators in an airplane cockpit. For the complex task of flying an airplane, pilots need detailed information about fuel, air speed, altitude, bearing, and other indicators that summarize the current and predicted environment. Reliance on one instrument can be fatal. Similarly, the complexity of managing an organization requires that managers be able to view performance in several areas simultaneously. A balanced scorecard—or a balanced set of measures—provides that valuable information.

MANAGING PERFORMANCE FROM THREE PERSPECTIVES A variety of studies have shown that both the public and private sectors have used balanced measures to help create high-performing organizations. Because balancing the perspectives of business, customers, and employees plays a key role in organizational success, OPM regulations (effective November 13, 2000) now require agencies to evaluate senior executive performance using balanced measures, which should take into account the following factors:

> **The business perspective,** which has a different interpretation in the Government than in the private sector. For many organizations, there are actually two separate sets of measures: the outcomes, or social/political impacts, which define the role of the agency/department within the Government and American society; and the business processes needed for organizational efficiency and effectiveness. Many of the outcome-oriented goals agencies establish in their strategic plans under the Government Performance and Results Act include the business perspective. To gain the business perspective, Federal managers must answer the question: *How do we look to Congress, the President, and other stakeholders?*

| **The customer perspective,** which considers the organization's performance through the eyes of its customers, i.e., American citizens, so that the organization retains a careful focus on customer needs and satisfaction. To achieve the best in business performance, agencies must incorporate customer needs and wants and must respond to them as part of their performance planning. Federal managers must answer the question: *How do customers see us?*

| **The employee perspective,** which focuses attention on the performance of the key internal  processes that drive the organization, including employee development and retention. This perspective directs attention to the basis of all future success—the organization's people and infrastructure. Adequate investment in these areas is critical to all long-term success. Federal managers must answer the question: *Do employees view the organization as a good place to work and develop their skills?*

TIE-IN TO EMPLOYEE PERFORMANCE  The balanced measures philosophy need not apply only at the organizational or senior executive level.  A balanced approach to employee performance appraisal is an effective way of getting a complete look at an employee's work performance. Too often, employee performance plans with their elements and standards measure behaviors, actions, or processes without also measuring the results of employees' work. By measuring only behaviors or actions in employee performance plans, an organization might find that most of its employees are appraised as *Outstanding* when the organization as a whole has failed to meet its objectives.

By using balanced measures at the organizational level, and by sharing the results with supervisors, teams, and employees, managers are providing the information needed to align employee performance plans with organizational goals. By balancing the measures used in employee performance plans, the performance picture becomes complete.

# Categories of Work

Sometimes performance plans describe elements using categories of work. Categories are classifications of work types often used to organize performance elements and standards. If, for example, the first beekeeper in our fable had used categories of work for his elements, he might have used the broad category of "making honey" as the element and then included a grouping that described all the activities the bees did to make the honey , such as gather nectar, report to the drones, etc. Other examples of categories of work and the types of activities that are often described under these categories include:

| customer service (greets customers with a smile, answers the phone promptly)

| teamwork (cooperates with others, shares information)

| communication (writes well, gives presentations)

| office duties (files papers, prepares reports)

**THIS HANDBOOK DOES NOT EXPLAIN HOW TO DESCRIBE AND MEASURE CATEGORIES OF WORK. HERE YOU ARE ASKED TO CONCENTRATE ON MEASURING ACCOMPLISHMENTS.**

## EXERCISE ON DISTINGUISHING ACTIVITIES FROM ACCOMPLISHMENTS:

It is time to check your understanding of the differences among activities, accomplishments, and categories. Please check the column that best describes each item.

| | ACCOMPLISHMENT | ACTIVITY | CATEGORY |
|---|---|---|---|
| Trains employees | | | |
| Supervision | | | |
| A completed case | | | |
| Public relations | | | |
| Recommendations | | | |
| Customer service | | | |
| HR policy interpretations | | | |
| Writes agency policy | | | |
| Solutions to problems | | | |
| Develops software programs | | | |
| Ideas and innovations | | | |
| Files paperwork | | | |
| Writes memos | | | |
| Computer systems that work | | | |
| Teamwork | | | |
| A completed project | | | |
| Satisfied customers | | | |
| Answers the phone | | | |
| Assists team members | | | |

ANSWERS ON PAGE 88

Y ou are now going to begin an eight-step process for developing
employee performance plans that support organizational goals. Before
you begin, however, we want to briefly review a process for developing
performance plans that you may have followed in the past but will **NOT**
be learning here.

Traditionally in some organizations, performance plans have been developed by copying the activities described in an employee's job description
onto the appraisal form. This handbook asks that you **NOT** begin with the
position description. Even though a performance plan must reflect the type
of work described in the employee's position description, the performance
plan does not have to mirror it.

The next two pages illustrate what happens when you develop a
performance plan solely from a position description. Page 22 is a
simplified position description for a Retirement Benefits Specialist
within the Claims Division branch of our example agency —
the Federal Benefits Bureau (FBB). Notice how the duties and
responsibilities in the position description all begin with a verb.
They describe **activities**, not **accomplishments**.

# chapter 3

A performance plan for a Retirement Benefits Specialist follows on page 23. It was written by copying the simplified position description from page 22 onto the appraisal form. Note that by copying the activities from the position description onto the appraisal form, FBB has developed a performance plan that only measures **activities**, not accomplishments. Also, by developing a performance plan without using a process that links **accomplishments** to organizational goals, the organization has lost the opportunity to use the appraisal process to communicate its goals to its employees and to align employee efforts with its goals.

REMEMBER THAT FBB'S APPRAISAL PROGRAM APPRAISES EMPLOYEE PERFORMANCE ON ELEMENTS AT FIVE LEVELS. THE FORM ON PAGE 23 SHOWS FIVE POSSIBLE LEVELS OF PERFORMANCE: UNSATISFACTORY (U), MINIMALLY SUCCESSFUL (MS), FULLY SUCCESSFUL (FS), EXCEEDS FULLY SUCCESSFUL (EFS), AND OUTSTANDING (O).

**POSITION DESCRIPTION**

*THE DUTIES AND RESPONSIBILITIES IN THE POSITION DESCRIPTION ALL BEGIN WITH A VERB. THEY DESCRIBE ACTIVITIES.*

---

POSITION DESCRIPTION: #123456
ORGANIZATIONAL TITLE: RETIREMENT BENEFITS SPECIALIST

---

**INTRODUCTION**

The incumbent of this position serves in a highly responsible capacity as a Retirement Benefits Specialist in an office responsible for the adjudication of claims for retirement and insurance benefits.

The work requires the services of an experienced, fully-trained Retirement Benefits Specialist. This position is responsible for considering and acting on all aspects of claims and applications for retirement and insurance benefits in an assigned area.

---

**MAJOR DUTIES AND RESPONSIBILITIES**

| Determine entitlement to and the amount of retirement annuities and survivor benefits, as well as payments to adult students and the entitlements and payments to certain other parties such as former spouses.

| Develop the record in individual cases, determining what is necessary and the sources of needed information.

| Adjudicate cases.

| Review and approve recommendations and decisions made by other Specialists, and provide training, advice, and assistance.

| Respond to inquiries from various customer sources and provide clear, responsive explanations of actions taken and the bases for them.

---

*APPROVING AUTHORITY SIGNATURE*                         *DATE*

**PERFORMANCE PLAN**

**X** *THIS IS **NOT** THE TYPE OF PERFORMANCE PLAN THAT YOU WILL DEVELOP IF YOU FOLLOW THE METHOD PRESENTED IN THIS HANDBOOK.*

### EMPLOYEE PERFORMANCE PLAN

| Name | Effective Date |
|---|---|

| JOB TITLE | NAME OF OFFICE |
|---|---|
| Retirement Benefits Specialist | Office of Retirement Services |

| ELEMENTS | TYPE | STANDARDS | RATING |
|---|---|---|---|
| *TECHNICAL AND POLICY EXPERT*<br><br>I Determine entitlement to and the amount of retirement annuities and survivor benefits, as well as payments to adult students and the entitlements and payments to certain other parties such as former spouses.<br><br>I Develop the record in individual cases, determining what is necessary and the sources of needed information.<br><br>I Adjudicate cases of unusual technical difficulty. | Critical | *FULLY SUCCESSFUL:*<br>Amounts of payments are accurate and determined timely.<br>Amounts of payments accurate and determined timely. | ☐ MS<br>☐ FS<br>☐ EFS<br>☐ O |
| *LEADERSHIP*<br><br>I Review and approve recommendations and decisions made by other Specialists, and provide advice and assistance. | Critical | *FULLY SUCCESSFUL:*<br>Reviews cases as required.<br>Provides high-quality feedback and advice to others. | ☐ U<br>☐ MS<br>☐ FS<br>☐ EFS<br>☐ O |
| *CUSTOMER SERVICE*<br><br>I Respond to inquiries from various customer sources and provide clear, responsive explanations of actions taken and the bases for them. | Critical | *FULLY SUCCESSFUL:*<br>Customer inquiries are routinely addressed accurately and in a timely fashion. | ☐ U<br>☐ MS<br>☐ FS<br>☐ EFS<br>☐ O |

COMMENTS:

| APPRAISING OFFICIAL SIGNATURE | EMPLOYEE SIGNATURE |
|---|---|

HAVING REVIEWED HOW TO DEVELOP A PERFORMANCE PLAN THAT FOCUSES ONLY ON ACTIVITIES, WE WILL NOW DEVELOP A PERFORMANCE PLAN THAT ESTABLISHES ELEMENTS AND STANDARDS, ADDRESSING ACCOMPLISHMENTS THAT LEAD TO ORGANIZATIONAL GOAL ACHIEVEMENT. **AN EIGHT-STEP PROCESS HAS BEEN DEVELOPED TO PRODUCE SUCH PLANS.** EACH STEP IN THE EIGHT-STEP PROCESS WE PRESENT IN THIS HANDBOOK BUILDS ON THE PREVIOUS STEP. YOU CANNOT SKIP A STEP AND END UP WITH GOOD RESULTS.

# step 1: look at the overall picture

## DEVELOPING EMPLOYEE PERFORMANCE PLANS

Instead of beginning at the bottom of the organization with the position description to develop employee performance plans, begin the process by looking at your agency's goals and objectives. Gather the following information:

**WHAT ARE YOUR AGENCY'S GENERAL OUTCOME GOALS AS OUTLINED IN ITS STRATEGIC PLAN?**
The Government Performance and Results Act of 1993 (i.e., GPRA) requires all agencies to develop a strategic plan that includes objective, quantifiable, and measurable performance goals. Agencies submitted their first strategic plans to Congress in September 1997. You will be referring to your agency's strategic plan while creating employee performance plans.

**WHAT ARE THE SPECIFIC PERFORMANCE GOALS ESTABLISHED FOR YOUR PROGRAM AREA AS OUTLINED IN YOUR AGENCY'S ANNUAL PERFORMANCE PLAN?**
GPRA also requires each agency to have an annual performance plan that sets out measurable goals that define what will be accomplished during a fiscal year. The goals in the annual performance plan describe the incremental progress toward achieving the general goals and objectives in the strategic plan. Performance plan goals are usually more specific and may be more output-oriented than the general outcome goals found in the strategic plan. Since performance plan goals should be used by managers as they direct and oversee how a program is carried out, these are the goals to which employee performance plans should be linked.

**WHAT PERFORMANCE MEASURES ARE ALREADY IN PLACE?**
You should be aware of the measurement systems that you can access for information on performance, including measures used for determining progress toward achieving Results Act goals and customer satisfaction surveys.

EXAMPLE OF ORGANIZATIONAL GOALS

Again, this handbook will continually refer to the Retirement Benefits Specialist position located within the Retirement Claims Division (a division of the Office of Retirement Services) of our example agency - the Federal Benefits Bureau (FBB). One of the primary functions of this position is to process retirement claims. FBB's strategic, outcome-oriented goals and two of the Office of Retirement Service's performance goals established in FBB's annual performance plan serve as examples of organizational goals. You will use this information in the next step of our eight-step process.

FBB's STRATEGIC GOALS

**Provide.** Offer a wide range of benefits and retirement services that will enhance recipients' quality of life.

**Diversity.** Create and maintain an inclusive work environment that values diversity and allows every employee the opportunity to reach their highest potential.

**Serve.** FBB's customer service, benefits, and retirement services meet the evolving needs of Federal employees and their families.

**Integrity.** Act as model agency within the Federal Government through fiscally responsible business practices and a commitment to excellence.

FBB'S ANNUAL PERFORMANCE PLAN GOALS FOR THE

OFFICE OF RETIREMENT SERVICES (ORS)

*ORS GOAL #2*

Retirement claims processing times are reduced and more customer services are delivered through self-servicing technology, while customer satisfaction is maintained at last fiscal year's level.

> **DIRECTLY LINKED TO FBB'S THIRD GOAL: SERVE**

*MEANS: [ONLY TWO MEANS ARE PRESENTED HERE.]*

- We will use the ORS Calculator implemented through the automation improvement project to reduce the time needed to process claims.
- We will continue the availability of both Interactive Voice Response and Internet technology to make annuity payment account changes.

*CUSTOMER SATISFACTION INDICATORS*

- Customers who received their first payment either before or when they expected. (The goal is to reach 80 percent.)
- Annuitants who indicate overall satisfaction with the handling of their retirement claims. (The goal is to reach 95 percent.)

*BUSINESS PROCESS INDICATORS*

- Interim payment processing time. (The goal is 4.5 days.)
- Annuity processing time. (The goal is 90 days.)
- Annuity claims accuracy. (The goal is 92 percent.)

*FINANCIAL INDICATOR*

Claims processing unit cost. (The goal is $190 per claim.)

The next step in this eight-step method is to determine the accomplishments (i.e., the products or services) of the work unit. Identifying work unit accomplishments lets you identify appropriate measures in the following steps of this process.

A work unit is a small group of employees that, in a traditional work structure, is supervised by the same first-line supervisor. Work units are generally the smallest organizational group on the organizational chart and usually include between 5 and 20 people. A work unit can also be a team—permanent or temporary—where the team members work interdependently toward a common goal.

Because not all types of work situations and structures are the same, this handbook offers three different ways to determine what to measure at the work unit level:

A.    A GOAL CASCADING METHOD

B.    A CUSTOMER-FOCUSED METHOD

C.    A WORK FLOW CHARTING METHOD

You can use one or all three methods, depending on what fits your situation. Whichever you use, remember to describe accomplishments (using nouns) rather than activities (using verbs).

# method A:
## cascade the agency's goals down to the work unit level

The **goal cascading method** works best for agencies with clear organizational goals and objectives, such as those established in the strategic plans and annual performance plans that agencies have prepared under the Government Performance and Results Act. This method requires answers to each of the following questions:

| **WHAT ARE THE AGENCY'S SPECIFIC GOALS AND OBJECTIVES?**
These can be found in the agency's annual performance plan and customer service standards. (Note that this question repeats Step 1 of the eight-step process.)

| **WHICH AGENCY GOAL(S) CAN THE WORK UNIT AFFECT?**
Often, work units may affect only one agency goal, but in some situations, agency goals are written so broadly that work units may affect more than one.

| **WHAT PRODUCT OR SERVICE DOES THE WORK UNIT PRODUCE OR PROVIDE TO HELP THE AGENCY REACH ITS GOALS?**
Clearly tying work unit products and services to organizational goals is key to this process. If a work unit finds it generates a product or service that does not affect organizational goals, the work unit needs to analyze the situation. It may decide to eliminate the product or service.

CASCADING AGENCY GOALS TO WORK UNITS

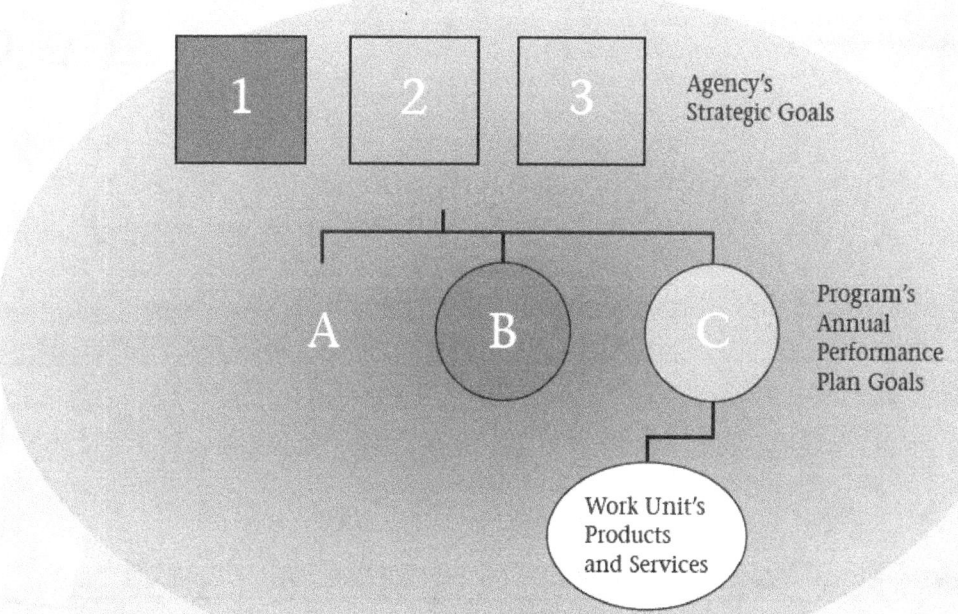

1   2   3   Agency's Strategic Goals

A   B   C   Program's Annual Performance Plan Goals

Work Unit's Products and Services

EXAMPLE OF CASCADING AGENCY GOALS TO A WORK UNIT

| | |
|---|---|
| *FBBStrategic Goal* | **FBB's THIRD GOAL: SERVE**<br><br>FBB's customer service, benefits, and retirement services meet the evolving needs of Federal employees and their families. |
| *An Office of Retirement Services (ORS) annual performance plan goal that cascades from FBB's THIRD GOAL: SERVE* | **ORS GOAL #2**<br><br>Retirement claims processing times are reduced and more customer services are delivered through self-servicing technology, while customer satisfaction is maintained at last fiscal year's levels. |
| *Some of Office of Retirement Services(ORS) GOALS* | A. Reduce overall processing times for annuity claims by processing fully developed annuity claims in an average of 90 days (re ORS Goal #2).<br><br>B. Reduce claims processing error rates by providing increased training in workplace competencies (re ORS Goal #2). |
| *Retirement Claims Division GOALS FBB* | • Claims processed in less time and with lower error rates.<br>• Increased number of individuals who can process insurance claims. |

## EXERCISE ON CASCADING GOALS

In the spaces below, begin mapping your agency's strategic and performance goals and how those goals cascade or "trickle down" through your organization. Try to show how your work unit's products or services link to your agency's goals. Remember to describe work unit accomplishments in terms of products or services (i.e., the end result of all the unit's activities).

*YOUR AGENCY'S GOALS*

*YOUR ORGANIZATION'S GOALS*

*YOUR WORK UNIT'S PRODUCTS OR SERVICES*

# method B:
## determine the products and services the work unit provides for its customers

The **customer-focused method** works well when there are no clear agency goals and when the work unit knows who its customers are and what they expect. Often this method is easier to apply to administrative work units that provide support functions, such as a human resources unit, an acquisitions unit, or a facilities maintenance unit. This method focuses on achieving customer satisfaction and requires answers to each of the following questions:

| Who are the customers of the work unit? If the work unit provides a support function, most of its customers may be internal to the agency.

| What products and/or services do the customers expect? Remember to describe accomplishments, not activities.

One way to approach this method is to build a map, as shown below. Place an oval representing the work unit in the center of a blank piece of paper. List the customer groups around the oval and describe the products or services the customers expect in the box under the customer groups.

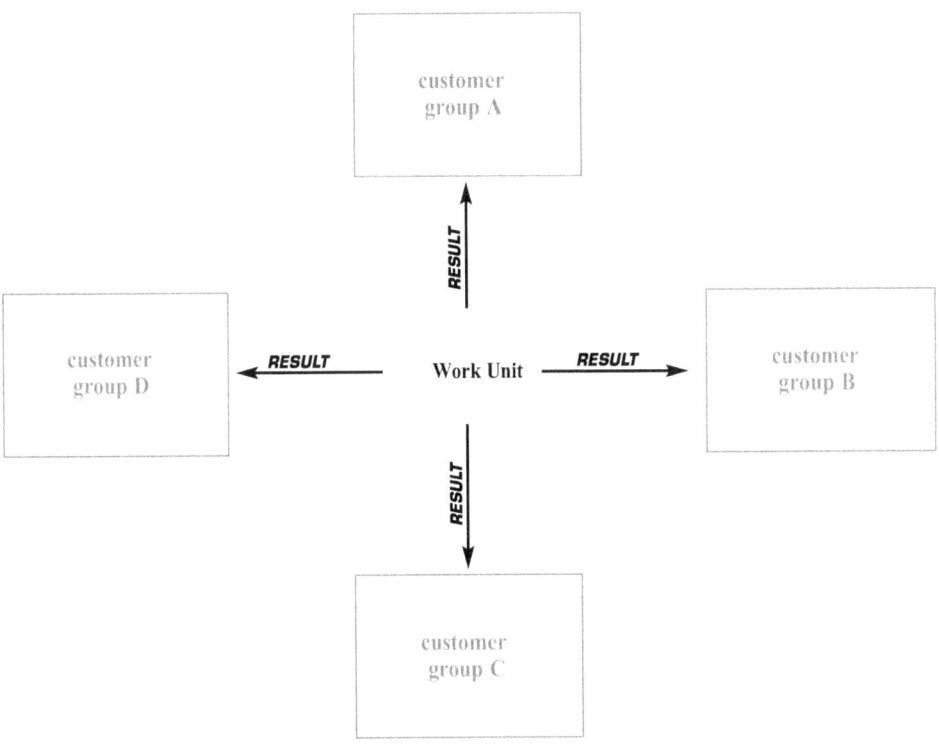

EXAMPLE OF IDENTIFYING CUSTOMERS AND THEIR EXPECTATIONS

The example below diagrams the accomplishments of the Office of Retirement Service's Claims Division from a customer-focused approach. Note that the accomplishments listed are the **results** of the team's work.

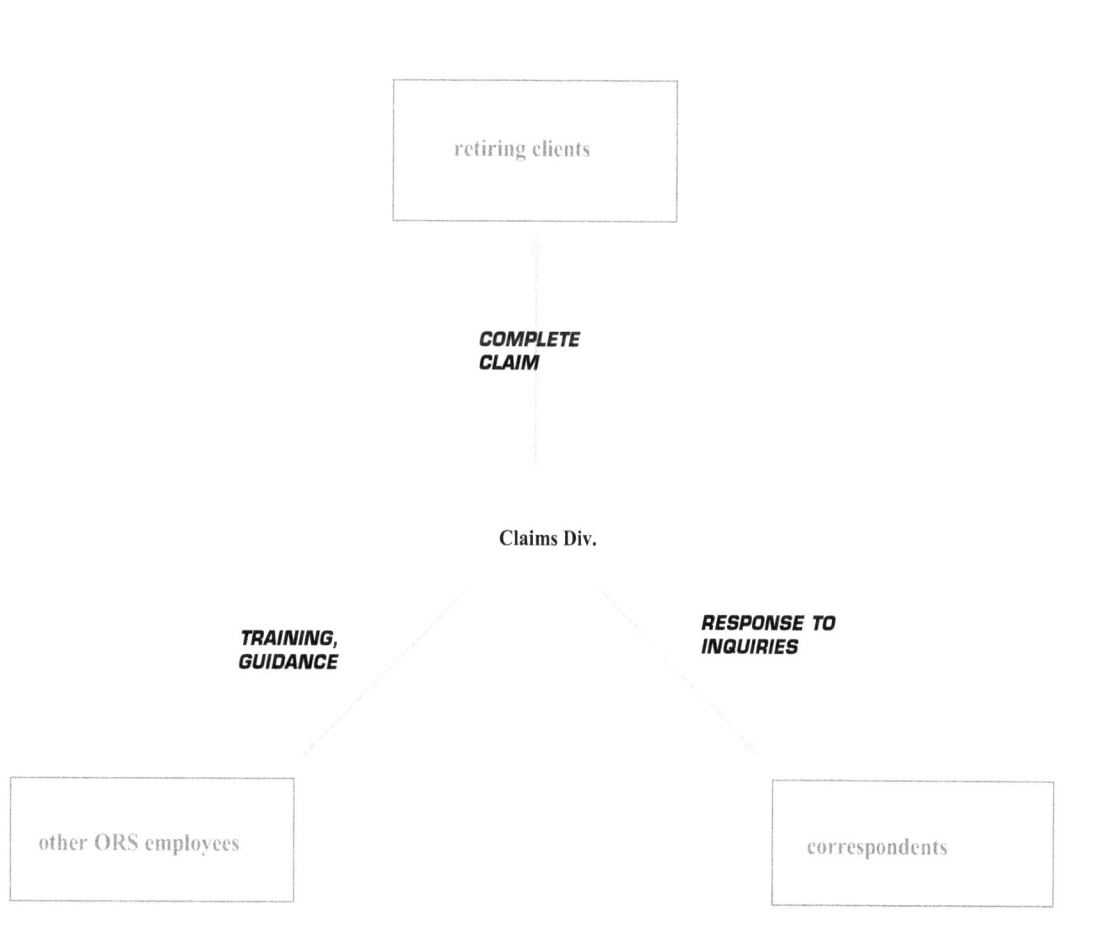

## EXERCISE FOR IDENTIFYING CUSTOMERS AND THEIR EXPECTATIONS

Use method B—the customer-focused method—to develop the product(s) or service(s) that your work unit provides.

1) Identify your work unit's customers

2) Determine what product(s) or service(s) your work unit supplies or provides to its customers

```
┌──────────────────┐
│  YOUR WORK UNIT  │
└──────────────────┘
```

# method C:
## develop a work flow chart for the work unit, establishing key steps in the work process

The **work flow charting method** works well for work units that are responsible for a complete work process, such as the processing of a case, the writing of a report, or the production of a customer information package. This method asks work units to develop work flow charts. A work flow chart is a picture of the major steps in a work process or project. It begins with the first step of the work process, maps out each successive step, and ends with the final product or service. To illustrate, the work flow chart to the right depicts a work process for building a house.

1. Foundation

2. Walls

3. Chimney

4. Roof

5. A complete house

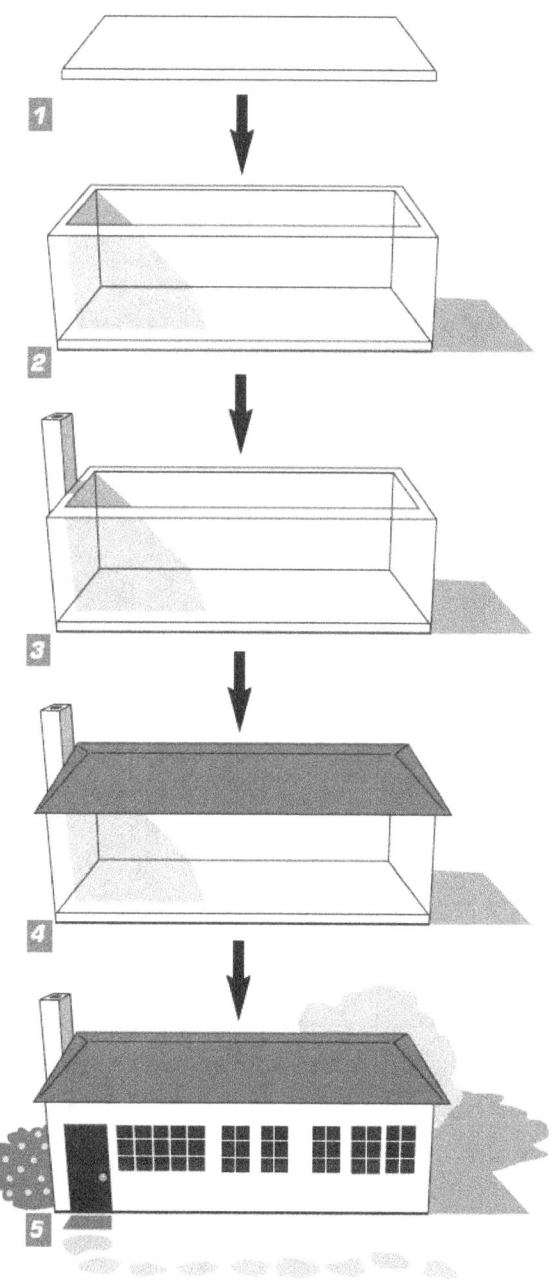

*TO HELP YOU BUILD YOUR WORK FLOW CHART, ANSWER THESE QUESTIONS:*

| How does the work unit produce its products or services? List the most basic steps in the process. For this purpose, you do not need to list all the activities required. (If you were analyzing the work to find ways of improving the process, you would need to list every activity.)

| Which are the most important steps in the process? By determining these steps, you highlight areas for performance measurement.

As you map out the process, you may find yourself describing activities. Try to group the activities into key steps by describing the results of those activities as one step in the process. As an example, the activities described in the following columns are all the activities that a publication team described when it was trying to create a work flow chart for the process of developing a newsletter. By grouping the related activities into the same columns, it was easier for the team to determine the results of those activities. Those results are written at the top of the column and became the key steps in the work flow chart.

## example method C

| RESULTS | PLAN FOR NEXT ISSUE | THE DRAFT VERSION OF THE ARTICLES | THE EDITED VERSION OF THE ARTICLE | THE CAMERA-READY COPY |
|---|---|---|---|---|
| ACTIVITIES | brainstorm ideas | interview contacts | review articles for errors | crop pictures |
| | meet to discuss ideas | get contact review and edits of article | make suggestions for improvements | develop the original graphics |
| | research various resources for ideas | get pictures or graphics, if used | make necessary changes | create layout boards |
| | get management approval of proposed plan | write article | consider the overall effect of the entire issue | format issue |

| *WORK FLOW CHART* | **PLAN FOR NEXT ISSUE** | **DRAFT ARTICLES** | **EDIT ARTICLES** | **CREATE CAMERA-COPY** |
|---|---|---|---|---|

## ANOTHER EXAMPLE OF WORK FLOW CHARTING

This example of the results of method C—which focuses on the work flow and the key steps in the work process—uses a work flow chart that maps the key steps in processing retirement claims. Notice that the steps are described as products. In other words, all the activities to complete the steps are not listed individually but have been grouped and described as products.

example method C

| | |
|---|---|
| Nondisability Claim Received | Annuity Computation |

An authorized first annuity payment is dispersed

An updated annuity roll master record → A completed and filed claim

## EXERCISE ON WORK FLOW CHARTING

1) Select a product or services that your work unit provides.

2) As best you can, map out the work process your unit uses. Focus on the major categories or steps of the work. You may need to first list the smaller steps of the work and then group them into subproducts. (Remember to describe products and services when you can, not activities.)

The performance elements that will be measured in the overall employee performance plan can include both individual and group assignments and responsibilities. The most important, results-oriented aspects of a unit's performance (which are its products or services) were identified in Step 2. (Other types of processes that work units may want to measure and include as elements in their plans—but which are not products or services and would not be identified through Step 2—include internal group dynamics processes, such as decision-making or problem-solving processes, or group/team development.)

Elements that address individual accomplishments can be identified using a role-results matrix. A role-results matrix is simply a table that identifies the results each work unit member must produce to support the unit's accomplishments. To build the matrix, list the work unit's products or services across the top row of a table. List each member of the work unit or each job position down the left column of the matrix. For each cell of the table, ask this question: What must this unit member produce or perform (i.e., accomplish) to support this particular work unit product or service? List those employee products or services (i.e., accomplishments) in the appropriate cell. The products or services you list for each unit member are possible performance elements that might be included in the employee's performance plan. All performance elements should be either quantifiable or verifiable and should be described as accomplishments (nouns), not activities (verbs).

### A ROLE-RESULTS MATRIX

| UNIT EMPLOYEES | UNIT PRODUCT OR SERVICE | UNIT PRODUCT OR SERVICE | UNIT PRODUCT OR SERVICE | UNIT PRODUCT OR SERVICE |
|---|---|---|---|---|
| EMPLOYEE 1 | ACCOMPLISHMENT | ACCOMPLISHMENT | ACCOMPLISHMENT | ACCOMPLISHMENT |
| EMPLOYEE 2 | ACCOMPLISHMENT | ACCOMPLISHMENT | ACCOMPLISHMENT | *N/A |
| EMPLOYEE 3 | ACCOMPLISHMENT | *N/A | ACCOMPLISHMENT | ACCOMPLISHMENT |
| EMPLOYEE 4 | *N/A | ACCOMPLISHMENT | ACCOMPLISHMENT | ACCOMPLISHMENT |

*The employee had no part in this work unit product or service.

## EXAMPLE OF A ROLE-RESULTS MATRIX

An example of a role-results matrix is shown below. It was built for a work team that produces a bimonthly policy newsletter. The team has five members: the editor, three writers, and a graphic artist. The final product or output is the newsletter. (The expected outcome is better educated employees.) The team created a work flow chart (see page 36), which identified four key steps in the work process. The team then used these key steps to build the matrix and will use it to develop performance elements.

Note that the main steps of the work process are laid out along the top of the matrix. The team members are listed down the left-hand column. Accomplishments are listed for each team member. Also, note that not all members have assignments or responsibilities for every team accomplishment. (This often will occur in cross-functional work units that include a variety of different job series.)

When building a role-results matrix, you may identify certain aspects of performance at either the work unit level or the individual level that you may not be able to measure (e.g., the effect a human resources program has on organizational performance) or over which the unit or the employee has no control (i.e., a portion of the product must be completed by someone outside the work unit). Also, certain aspects of performance may cost too much to measure or the agency may not have the resources to measure them. You should not include these aspects of performance as elements in the performance plan, but they are still legitimate parts of the role-results matrix.

A role-results matrix is a valuable management tool. When supervisors involve employees in the process of completing the matrix, everyone's role in the work unit is very clear, which is important to the successful performance of the group. The whole process of determining work unit products and services, and then completing a role-results matrix, is a beneficial team-building exercise.

example role-results matrix

**A ROLE-RESULTS MATRIX FOR A NEWSLETTER TEAM:**

TEAM ACCOMPLISHMENTS

| TEAM MEMBERS | THE PLAN FOR THE NEXT ISSUE | THE DRAFT VERSION OF THE ARTICLES | THE EDITED VERSION OF THE ARTICLES | THE CAMERA-READY COPY |
|---|---|---|---|---|
| **EDITOR** | TOPICS TO BE COVERED | | ARTICLES THAT HAVE BEEN EDITED | |
| **WRITER A** | RECOMMENDATIONS FOR ARTICLES | DRAFT ARTICLE(S) | | |
| **WRITER B** | RECOMMENDATIONS FOR ARTICLES | DRAFT ARTICLE(S) | | |
| **WRITER C** | RECOMMENDATIONS FOR ARTICLES | DRAFT ARTICLE(S) | | |
| **GRAPHIC ARTIST** | RECOMMENDATIONS FOR LAYOUT | | | A CAMERA-READY COPY |

## ANOTHER EXAMPLE OF A ROLE-RESULTS MATRIX

The table below displays example data gathered for FBB's Office of Retirement Service's Claims Division using the cascading method as described on pages 29-30 and the customer-focused method on pages 33-34. Note that the products or services (i.e., the work unit accomplishments) identified through the process of Step 2 are shown along the top of the matrix. Employees are listed down the left side of the matrix. Employee work accomplishments are included in each cell. Notice that the employee work responsibilities are described as accomplishments (i.e., products or services) rather than activities or behaviors.

| EMPLOYEES | WORK UNIT PRODUCTS OR SERVICES | | |
|---|---|---|---|
| *DIVISION MGR\** | *CLAIMS PROCESSED IN LESS TIME AND WITH LOWER ERROR RATES* | *RESPONSES TO INQUIRIES* | *INCREASED NUMBER OF EMPLOYEES WHO CAN PROCESS CLAIMS* |
| *RETIREMENT BENEFITS SPECIALIST* | A COMPLETED **CLAIM**<br><br>**SUGGESTION(S)** FOR IMPROVING THE PROCESS | N/A | **GUIDANCE,** TRAINING, AND **TECHNICAL ASSISTANCE** TO OTHER SPECIALISTS |
| *CUSTOMER SERVICE SPECIALISTS* | CLAIM CONTROL **LOG** | **CORRESPONDENCE** THAT IS FORMATTED, MAILED, AND FILED<br><br>**ANSWERS** TO CUSTOMER TELEPHONE QUESTIONS | N/A |

*\*Note that the Division Manager is on the same row as work unit accomplishments. This shows that the Branch Manager is responsible for work unit results.*

## EXERCISE FOR BUILDING A ROLE-RESULTS MATRIX

Fill in the role-results matrix for your work unit. Place the work unit products or services that you developed in Step 2 (using method A, page 31, method B, page 34, and/or method C, page 38) along the top of the matrix. Fill in the names or the job titles of the work unit's employees in the left-hand column. Then fill in the employees' accomplishments that contribute to each work unit accomplishment.

| EMPLOYEES | WORK UNIT PRODUCTS OR SERVICES | | | |
|---|---|---|---|---|
| ORGANIZATIONAL CHIEF | | | | |
| | | | | |
| | | | | |
| | | | | |

In Steps 2 and 3 of the process presented in this handbook, you developed the expected accomplishments for the work unit and the unit's employees. Now, in Step 4, you will:

| identify which accomplishment(s) should be included as elements in the performance plan

| select which type of element to use

| assign weights or priorities

All employees must have at least one critical element in their performance plan. Critical elements must address individual performance only, except in the case of supervisors who may be held responsible for a work unit's products or services. Work unit performance can be addressed through non-critical or additional performance elements. In appraisal programs with only two summary levels, work unit performance can be addressed only through additional performance elements.

Once you have classified elements as either critical, non-critical, or additional, and if your appraisal program allows, prioritize them so that work units and employees know which elements are most important. One way to do this is to distribute 100 percentage points across the elements based on each one's importance to the organization. (Programs usually allocate weights in five-percent increments.)

## HOW CAN YOU DETERMINE WHICH ELEMENTS ARE CRITICAL?

Remember that critical elements are work assignments or responsibilities of such importance that unacceptable performance on the element would result in a determination that an employee's overall performance is unacceptable. Defining critical elements must be done thoughtfully because an employee's unacceptable performance on any critical element could be the basis for an adverse action. To help decide whether an element should be classified as critical or not, answer the following questions:

| Is the element a major component of the work? If you answered "yes," the element might be critical.

| Does the element address individual performance only? Elements measuring group performance cannot be critical elements, except as explained for supervisors and only under certain circumstances.

| If the employee performed unacceptably on the element, would there be serious consequences to completing the work of the organization? If employee error on the element affects the work unit's accomplishments, the element may be critical.

| Does the element require a significant amount of the employee's time? If you answered "yes," the element might be critical.

Unless prescribed by your appraisal program, there is no fixed or uniform number of critical elements to be included in the performance plan; the number varies with the work assignments and may vary from year to year in response to changing program emphases. However, every employee must have at least one critical element.

## EXAMPLE OF IDENTIFYING ELEMENTS

The Claims Division within the Office of Retirement Services (ORS) has been used on the following page as an example for identifying elements. The expected accomplishments of the Retirement Benefits Specialist (as outlined in the role-results matrix on page 41) are listed down the left side of the matrix on the next page. The work unit accomplishments for the Division are also listed. The next column shows how the Division Manager and employees designated elements as critical, non-critical, or additional. Finally, priority points are assigned to each element to give them relative weights. (Remember that ORS's appraisal program uses five levels to appraise employee performance on elements and summarizes performance overall at five levels and that non-critical and additional performance elements are allowed.)

# example identifying elements

Note the following in the matrix on page 45:

1. The Division decided that "Suggestions for Improving the Process" should not affect the summary level, but the Division wanted to track and measure the value of the suggestions in order to recognize individuals who help improve the process. Therefore, it was included as an additional element and given a weight of 0. The Division plans to use the results of performance on this element as a criterion for awards recognizing innovation by individuals within ORS.

2. The Division decided that claims completed by individuals should be a critical element for Benefits Specialists, but the Division also felt it was important to count in employee performance plans the group's performance as a whole on claims completed. The Division felt that counting group performance on claims processed would encourage specialists to work together as a group and promote collaboration. Since this Division is under a five-level appraisal program and it wants to count this group element in the appraisal process, it will be a non-critical element. (If it were in a two-level appraisal program, the group element would have to be an additional performance element.)

3. For the group goal of increased number of employees who can process insurance claims, the Division decided not to count group performance in the appraisal process. Because of the importance of this group goal, however, management decided to make it an additional element and use it as a basis for recognizing the group if it meets specific goals. (Note that the Division is measuring individual performance to support this group goal and is counting individual performance as a critical element.)

4. The Division determined the priority of each element by distributing 100 points across the critical and non-critical elements. The priority points let employees know which elements are more important to the organization. Priority points also are used in this example to affect how the summary level will be determined. Using this method allows non-critical elements to count significantly in the summary level determination. (Failure on the non-critical element would not cause performance to be *Unacceptable*; it would merely count as 0 priority points and could lower the summary level—but not to *Unacceptable*.)

**ORS RETIREMENT CLAIMS DIVISION**
**RETIREMENT BENEFITS SPECIALIST**

| ELEMENT | ELEMENT TYPE | WEIGHT or POINTS |
|---|---|---|
| \| Completed claims | Critical (CE) | 50 |
| \| Suggestion(s) for improving the process | Additional (AE) | 0 |
| \| Guidance and technical assistance to other specialists | Critical (CE) | 35 |
| **WORK PRODUCTS OR SERVICES** | | |
| Claims processed in less time and with lower error rates | Non-critical (NC) | 15 |
| Increased number of employees who can process claims | Additional (AE) | 0 |

## EXERCISE ON IDENTIFYING ELEMENTS

Based on the accomplishments that you identified for your job in the role-results matrix that you made on page 42 and working within the rules established by your appraisal program, identify appropriate elements and categorize them as critical, non-critical, and, if appropriate, additional performance elements. Write those elements and their type under the columns marked "Element" and "Type" on the foldout form on the back cover. (If you have a two-level appraisal program—that is, a pass/fail program—you cannot use non-critical elements.) If applicable, prioritize the elements by distributing 100 points among the elements, giving more points to elements that are more important. Write the priority points you assign under the column labeled "priority" on the foldout form on the back cover .

**FOLD OVER INSIDE BACK COVER FLAP AS SHOWN TO FILL OUT CHART**

In Step 4 of this process, you designated the critical, non-critical, and additional performance elements you will include in your performance plan. In Step 5, you will determine how to measure performance on those elements.

Measures are the yardsticks used to determine how well work units and employees produced or provided products or services. To develop specific measures of performance for each element in your performance plan, you first must determine the general measures that apply to each. Once you determine the general and specific measures, you will be able to develop the standards for your elements, which you will do in Step 6 of this process. Your standards will be worded in terms of the specific measures developed in this step.

The performance pyramid below shows the types of general measures that are used at different levels in the organization. Note that the balanced measures incorporating the business, customer, and employee perspectives are appropriate for measuring managerial performance and are sometimes appropriate for supervisory or even work unit performance. At the bottom of the pyramid, the four general measures normally used for measuring work unit and employee performance are quality, quantity, timeliness, and cost-effectiveness.

PERFORMANCE PYRAMID FOR IDENTIFYING PERFORMANCE MEASURES

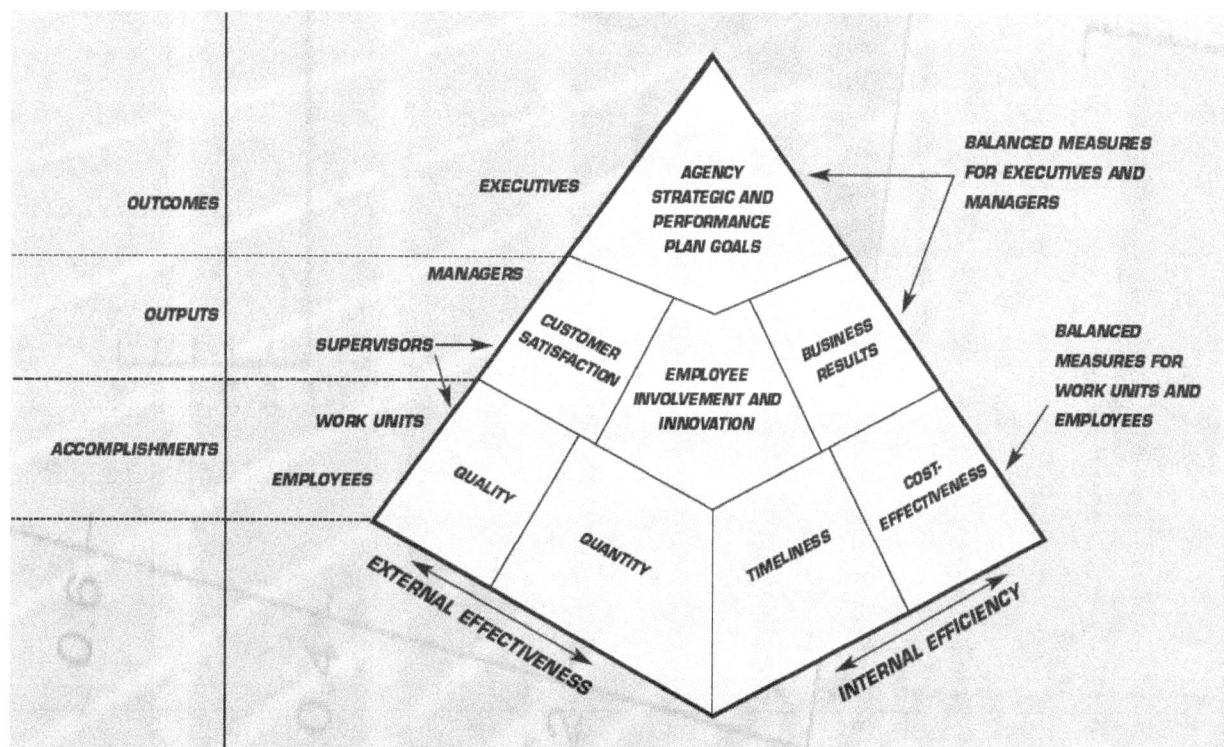

## GENERAL MEASURES

QUALITY addresses how well the employee or work unit performed the work and/or the accuracy or effectiveness of the final product. Quality refers to accuracy, appearance, usefulness, or effectiveness. Quality measures can include error rates (such as the number or percentage of errors allowable per unit of work) and customer satisfaction rates (determined through a customer survey).

QUANTITY addresses how much work the employee or work unit produced. Quantity measures are expressed as a number of products produced or services provided, or as a general result to achieve.

TIMELINESS addresses how quickly, when, or by what date the employee or work unit produced the work.

COST-EFFECTIVENESS addresses dollar savings or cost control for the Government. You should develop measures that address cost-effectiveness on specific resource levels (money, personnel, or time) that you can generally document and measure in agency annual fiscal year budgets. Cost-effectiveness measures may include such aspects of performance as maintaining or reducing unit costs, reducing the time it takes to produce or provide a product or service, or reducing waste.

## DEVELOPING SPECIFIC MEASURES

To develop specific measures, you first must determine the general measure(s) that are important for each element (i.e., quantity, quality, timeliness, or cost-effectiveness). Then, determine how to measure the quantity, quality, timeliness, and/or cost-effectiveness for the element. If you can measure an accomplishment with numbers, record the form of measurement. If you can only describe performance (i.e., observe and verify), clarify who will appraise the performance and the factors they will appraise.

The kinds of questions you should ask in this process include the following.

FIRST: For each element, decide which general measures apply:

- Is quality important? Does the stakeholder or customer care how well the work is done?

- Is quantity important? Does the stakeholder or customer care how many are produced?

- Is it important to accomplish the element by a certain time or date?

- Is it important to accomplish the element within certain cost limits?

- What measures are already available?

SECOND: For each general measure, ask:

- How could [quality, quantity, timeliness, and/or cost-effectiveness] be measured?

- Is there some number or percent that could be tracked?

If the element does not lend itself to being measured with numbers and can only be described, ask:

- Who could judge that the element was done well?

- What factors would they look for?

FINALLY: Write down or otherwise record the specific measures. If the measure is numeric, list the units that you will track. If the measure is descriptive, identify the judge and list the factors that the judge will look for to observe and verify performance.

## CLAIMS DIVISION

Note that general and specific measures have been added to the elements for a Retirement Benefits Specialist (see page 45).

Also note that only the measures have been identified, not the standard that describes how well the element should be done. (Standards are addressed in the next step in the process.)

RETIREMENT BENEFITS SPECIALIST

| PRIORITY POINTS | ELEMENT | TYPE | GENERAL MEASURES | SPECIFIC MEASURES |
|---|---|---|---|---|
| 50 | Completed *claim* | CE | Quality<br><br>Quantity<br>Timeliness | The accuracy of annuity amounts.<br>The completeness of the paperwork<br>The number of claims processed per week<br>The average number of days it takes to process a claim* |
| 35 | *Guidance* and *technical assistance* to other specialists | CE | Quality<br><br><br><br><br>Timeliness | The accuracy of the information, as determined by supervisor<br>The perceptions of other specialists that the incumbent is willing to assist and that feedback is helpful<br>The number of hours it takes for the incumbent to respond to other specialists' requests for assistance |
| 15 | **Division Element:** Division *claims* processed in less time and with lower error rates | NC | Quality<br><br>Quantity<br><br>Timeliness | The accuracy rate for annuity amounts from the whole Division<br>The number of claims the Division processes per week<br>The average number of days it takes to process a claim* |
| 0 | Suggestion(s) for improving the process (for special individual recognition) | AE | Quality<br><br><br><br>Quantity<br>Cost-Effectiveness | The supervisor's and reviewers' judgment that the suggestion(s) improve(s) efficiency, productivity, and flexibility<br>The number of suggestions made<br>The amount of money saved by adopting the suggestion |
| 0 | **Division Element:** Increased number of employees who can process claims | AE | Quantity<br><br>Quality | The number of employees who can do claims<br>The accuracy rate of annuities processed |

*Note: Using the average adjusts for the varying levels of difficulty in claims and ensures that specialists will not focus only on easy claims and ignore the difficult ones. Also, all specialists are assigned equal numbers of easy and difficult claims to ensure fairness of the standard. Finally, the average can be prorated when necessary.

## EXERCISE FOR DETERMINING GENERAL AND SPECIFIC MEASURES

Determine the general measures for your job based on the elements that you created in the previous exercise on page 46. Next, identify some specific measures. Write down those general and specific measures under the columns labeled "General Measure" and "Specific Measure" on the foldout form on the back cover.

**FOLD OVER INSIDE BACK COVER FLAP AS SHOWN TO FILL OUT CHART**

# step 6:
# develop work unit and
# individual standards

The next step in the process of developing a performance plan is to establish standards for the elements. To work through this section successfully, you will need to know the number of levels your appraisal program uses to appraise elements. You also will need to know which performance level your program uses as the retention standard. (A definition of retention standard is included in this section.) The discussions below address performance standards and what to avoid when writing standards.

## WHAT IS A PERFORMANCE STANDARD?

Performance standards are management-approved expressions of the performance threshold(s), requirement(s), or expectation(s) that employees must meet to be appraised at particular levels of performance.

Each critical element must have a *Fully Successful* or equivalent standard established. Technically, neither non-critical elements nor additional performance elements require a *Fully Successful* or equivalent standard. However, to help employees and work units understand the expectations for performance on these elements, we recommend that they have a clear idea of what is considered fully successful performance.

[NOTE: NON-CRITICAL ELEMENTS MUST BE APPRAISABLE AT LEAST ON TWO LEVELS, BUT THOSE LEVELS CAN BE ESTABLISHED HIGHER THAN THE FULLY SUCCESSFUL LEVEL.)

## WHAT SHOULD PERFORMANCE STANDARDS INCLUDE?

Once you have established the specific measures that apply to the elements, you can begin to write the standards. Before writing the *Fully Successful* standard, you must know the number of levels that your appraisal program uses to appraise elements. For example, if you are under an appraisal program that uses two levels to appraise elements, the *Fully Successful* standard would describe a single point of performance. Any performance at or above that point is *Fully Successful,* and anything below it is *Unacceptable.* If, however, your appraisal program uses five levels to appraise performance, you would describe the *Fully Successful* standard as a range. Performance that exceeds the top of that range would be appraised at the level(s) above *Fully Successful,* and performance below the bottom of that range would be *Minimally Successful* (or equivalent) or *Unacceptable.* How you write the *Fully Successful* standard depends on the number of levels your program uses to appraise performance on elements.

If a specific measure for an element is numeric, for example, you would list the units to be tracked and determine the range of numbers (or the single number in a program that appraises elements at two levels) that represents *Fully Successful* performance. If the specific measure is descriptive, you would identify the appraiser(s) who would judge performance, list the factors that the appraiser(s) would look for, and determine what he or she would see or report that verifies that *Fully Successful* performance for that element had been met. (Remember to express performance standards in terms of the specific measure[s] determined in Step 5 of this process.)

Several examples of elements and standards are included below. The specific measures are in italics; the performance (or range of performance) that actually establishes the level of the standard is in boldface type.

## ELEMENT: CASES COMPLETED

**Fully Successful Standard** in an appraisal program that appraises elements at five levels (to meet this standard, all of the bullets listed must be present or occur):

| no more than **3-4** *valid customer complaints per year*, as determined by the supervisor

| no more than **2-3** *errors per quarter*, as spotted by the supervisor

| no more than **4-5** *late cases per year* (processed later than 10 working days from receipt)

(If this standard had been written for an appraisal program that appraised elements at only two levels, the standard would have been "no more than **4** *valid customer complaints per year,*" "no more than **3** *errors per quarter,*" and "no more than **5** *late cases per year.*")

## ELEMENT: MEETINGS SCHEDULED

**Fully Successful Standard** in an appraisal program that appraises elements at five levels (to meet this standard, all of the bullets listed must be present or occur):

The **meeting leader and attendees generally are satisfied** that

| *the room size matched the group size*

| *attendees were notified of the meeting*

| *attendees knew whom to call for information*

| *the meeting was set up by the deadline*

## ELEMENT: LEGAL ADVICE

**Fully Successful Standard** in an appraisal program that appraises elements at five levels (to meet this standard, all of the bullets listed must be present or occur):

| Consistent with attorney's grade, attorney **usually** *carries an adequate workload of projects*, **frequently** *takes on new projects* to meet the needs of the office, and **generally** *shows personal initiative* in handling projects (generally, projects are of average difficulty)

| Consistent with attorney's grade, legal advice rendered is **infrequently** *modified by practice group leaders and supervisors* in a **significant** way

| Advice given to clients is **usually** *timely and thorough* and of **average** *quality*, and **usually** *shows sensitivity* to program and agency needs

*ADDITIONAL EXAMPLES OF ELEMENTS AND STANDARDS SPECIFICALLY WRITTEN FOR APPRAISAL PROGRAMS THAT APPRAISE ELEMENTS AT FIVE, THREE, AND TWO LEVELS ARE INCLUDED IN THE APPENDICES.*

## WHAT SHOULD YOU AVOID WHEN WRITING RETENTION STANDARDS?

By "retention" standard, we mean the standard that describes the level of performance necessary to be retained in a job (i.e., the standard written for performance one level above the *Unacceptable* level). In appraisal programs that do not have a *Minimally Successful* or equivalent level available for appraising elements, the retention-level standard is the *Fully Successful* standard. Otherwise, the retention standard is the *Minimally Successful* or equivalent standard.

The Merit Systems Protection Board (MSPB) and the courts have issued many decisions on the topic of valid performance standards. This section highlights what the Board deems to be two major errors to avoid when writing standards. In order to avoid reversal by the MSPB, agencies must ensure that "retention" standards:

- are not impermissibly absolute (i.e., allow for some error)
- inform the employee of the level of performance needed to retain his or her job

### AVOID ABSOLUTE RETENTION STANDARDS

An "absolute" retention standard—one that allows for no errors—is acceptable only in very limited circumstances. When a single failure to perform under a critical element would result in loss of life, injury, breach of national security, or great monetary loss, an agency can legitimately defend its decision to require perfection from its employees. In other circumstances, the MSPB and the courts usually will find that the agency abused its discretion by establishing retention standards that allow for no margin of error.

When writing standards, you should avoid the appearance of requiring perfection at the retention level. In appraisal programs that do not appraise elements at the *Minimally Successful* or equivalent level, you must carefully word the *Fully Successful* or equivalent standards so that they are not absolute. For example here are *Fully Successful* standards used by agencies that the MSPB would consider absolute retention standards if they were used in a two-level appraisal program:

- Work is timely, efficient, and of acceptable quality
- Communicates effectively within and outside of the organization

MSPB considers these standards absolute because they appear to require that work is *always* timely, efficient, and of acceptable quality and that the employee *always* communicates effectively. When writing standards—especially retention standards—avoid simply listing tasks without describing the regularity of the occurrence of the task—but also avoid the requirement to do it *always*.

Also, in appraisal programs that appraise elements at levels above *Fully Successful*, the *Fully Successful* standard itself—as well as the *Exceeds Fully Successful* standard when an *Outstanding* or equivalent level is possible—should not be absolute. If it is supposed to be possible to exceed, make sure it is written that way.

To help determine whether you are writing an absolute standard, ask yourself:

| How many times may the employee fail this requirement and still be acceptable?

| Does the retention standard use words such as "all," "never," and "each"?  (These words do not automatically create an absolute standard, but they often alert you to problems.)

| If the retention standard allows for no errors, would it be valid according to the criteria listed above (risk of death, injury, etc.)?

The examples of elements and standards included in the appendices were carefully written to avoid absolute requirements.

### AVOID "BACKWARD" STANDARDS

Case law requires that an employee understand the level of performance needed for retention in the position.  When using a *Minimally Successful* level of performance, a common tendency is to describe it in terms of work that does not get done instead of what must be done to meet that retention standard.  Describing negative performance actually describes *Unacceptable* performance.  Standards such as "fails to meet deadlines" or "performs work inaccurately" allow an employee to do virtually no work or to do it poorly and still meet that retention standard. MSPB considers these "backward" retention standards invalid.  To help you determine whether you are writing a backward retention standard, ask:

| Does the standard express the level of work the supervisor wants to see or does it describe negative performance? (Example of describing negative performance: Requires assistance more than 50 percent of the time.)

| If the employee did nothing, would he or she meet the standard, as written? (Example: Completes fewer than four products per year.)

## MORE EXAMPLE STANDARDS

Example standards for a Retirement Benefits Specialist are shown on the next two pages. These standards were written for elements that are appraised at five levels. The appraisal regulations only require that a *Fully Successful* standard be established for each element. However, to clarify at the outset what employees need to do to exceed the *Fully Successful* level (as well as what they must do to be retained in the position) the Claims Division includes standards for the *Minimally Successful, Fully Successful,* and *Exceeds Fully Successful* levels of performance. (Performance below the minimum of the *Minimally Successful* range of performance is considered *Unacceptable,* and performance above the maximum of the *Exceeds Fully Successful* range of performance is *Outstanding.*)

Most of the example standards on the next two pages are quantifiable. The numbers used are based on work flow data. Examples of descriptive standards written at a variety of levels are found in the appendices. In all these examples, distinguishing between *Fully Successful* and levels above or below *Fully Successful* requires careful planning and forethought.

NOTE THAT THE STANDARDS TYPICALLY DESCRIBE A RANGE OF PERFORMANCE. ALSO NOTE THAT THE ELEMENTS HAVE BEEN REARRANGED TO ORDER THE ELEMENTS BY WEIGHT.

*RETIREMENT BENEFITS SPECIALIST*

| ELEMENT | GENERAL MEASURES | SPECIFIC MEASURES | STANDARDS* | | |
|---|---|---|---|---|---|
| | | | MINIMALLY SUCCESSFUL | FULLY SUCCESSFUL | EXCEEDS FULLY SUCCESSFUL |
| Completed *claims*<br><br>⎪ Critical Element<br><br>⎪ 50 priority points | Quality | The accuracy of annuity amounts<br><br>The completeness of the paperwork | 82-87% of annuity amounts are accurate and of claims are complete | 88-93% of annuity amounts are accurate and of claims are complete | 94-97% of annuity amounts are accurate and of claims are complete |
| | Quantity | The number of claims processed per week | 10-12 claims processed per week | 13-16 claims processed per week | 17-20 claims processed per week |
| | Timeliness | The average number of days it takes to process a claim | An average of 101-110 days to complete claim | An average of 90-100 days to complete claim | An average of 75-90 days to complete claim |
| *Guidance* and *technical assistance* to other specialists<br><br>⎪ Critical Element<br><br>⎪ 35 priority points | Quality | The accuracy of the information, as determined by supervisor<br><br>The perceptions of other specialists that the incumbent is willing to assist and that feedback is helpful | Usually accurate<br><br><br>50-59% of specialists agree that incumbent is routinely willing to assist and that feedback is helpful | Usually accurate<br><br><br>60-80% of specialists agree that incumbent is routinely willing to assist and that feedback is helpful | Almost always accurate<br><br>81-89% of specialists agree that incumbent is routinely willing to assist and that feedback is helpful |
| | Timeliness | The number of hours it takes for the incumbent to respond to other specialists' requests for assistance | Usually responds within 9-12 working hours from receipt of request | Usually responds within 4-8 working hours from receipt of request | Usually responds within 2-3 working hours from receipt of request |
| **Claims Division:** *claims* processed in less time and with lower error rates<br><br>⎪ Non-critical Element<br><br>⎪ 15 priority points | Quality | The accuracy rate for annuity amounts from the whole Division | N/A** | 88-93% annuity amounts are accurate | 94-97 % annuity amounts are accurate |
| | Quantity | The number of claims the Division processes per week | | 220-230 claims processed by the Division per week | 231-244 claims processed by the Division per week |
| | Timeliness | The average number of days it takes to process a claim | | An average of 90-100 days to complete claim | An average of 75-90 days to complete claim |

*RETIREMENT BENEFITS SPECIALIST, CONTINUED*

| ELEMENT | GENERAL MEASURES | SPECIFIC MEASURES | STANDARDS* | | |
| --- | --- | --- | --- | --- | --- |
| | | | MINIMALLY SUCCESSFUL | FULLY SUCCESSFUL | EXCEEDS FULLY SUCCESSFUL |
| Suggestion(s) for improving the process (for special individual recognition) | Quality | The supervisor's and reviewers' judgment that the suggestion(s) improve(s) efficiency, productivity, and flexibility | N/A** | Management and Division members determine that the suggestion(s) is/are worth adopting | Management and Division members determine that the suggestion(s) is/are worth adopting |
| ‖ Additional Performance Element | Quantity | The number of suggestions made | | Incumbent provides 1-2 adopted suggestions per year | Incumbent provides 3-5 adopted suggestions per year |
| ‖ 0 priority points | Cost Effectiveness | The amount of money saved by adopting the suggestion | | The incumbent's suggestion saved up to 10% of costs | The incumbent's suggestion saved 10-25% of costs |
| **Claims Division:** Increased number of employees who can process claims | Quantity | The number of employees who can do claims | N/A** | 35- 50% of Division employees can process claims | 51-75% of Division employees can process claims |
| ‖ Additional Performance Element | Quality | The accuracy rate of annuities processed | | 88-93% of annuity amounts are accurate | 94-97% of annuity amounts are accurate |
| ‖ 0 priority points | | | | | |

*To meet the performance level of the standards described for each element, each listed part of the standard must be present or occur.

**The Division decided that there was no benefit to establishing a *Minimally Successful* standard for a non-critical or an additional performance element.

If these standards had been written for an appraisal program that appraises elements at only two levels, only the *Fully Successful* standard would have been included and it would describe a single point, not a range. So, for example, on the first element (i.e., completed case files) instead of establishing an 88-93 percent accuracy rate, etc., as the *Fully Successful* standard, the standard would be:

‖ 88% accuracy or better

‖ at least 13 cases processed per week;

‖ takes an average of 100 days to complete case

Another point of interest in the example is that the elements and standards written for the Division were included in each Division employee's performance plan as group elements and standards.

## EXERCISE FOR WRITING STANDARDS

Based on the elements and measures you established in the previous exercise on page 51, develop *Fully Successful* standards for your elements. Write those standards under the column labeled "Standards" on the foldout form on the back cover. Remember to write standards that specifically match the measurement levels of your appraisal program (i.e., two-level or more than two-level). This exercise is asking you to develop only the *Fully Successful* standard. However, if your appraisal program appraises elements at more than two levels, you may also want to define the other levels of performance that are possible.

**FOLD OVER INSIDE BACK COVER FLAP AS SHOWN TO FILL OUT CHART**

# step 7:
# determine how to monitor performance

Monitoring performance means measuring performance and providing feedback to employees. Agency appraisal programs are required to provide ongoing appraisal, which includes, but is not limited to, conducting one or more progress reviews during each appraisal period. In addition to a once- or twice-a-year progress review, which is sometimes a formal part of the appraisal process, supervisors and employees should discuss performance informally and often.

Determining how to monitor performance is an important step in developing performance plans. You may have worked through the previous six steps of the process presented in this handbook, developed what you thought were great elements and standards, and then found that monitoring performance on an element is impossible, or too costly, or too time-consuming. If this happens, think through other specific measures that indicate performance—measures that are as specific as possible.

To complete this step in the process:

| Determine what data to collect for each performance element, the source of the data, and whether to collect all the data or just a sample

| Determine when to collect the data, who will collect it, and who will receive it

| Review existing reports for possible use as feedback reports

| Create feedback tables or graphs where necessary or applicable

| Try to design feedback processes that give feedback automatically

## FEEDBACK

Effective and timely feedback addressing employee performance on elements and standards is an essential component of a successful performance management program. People need to know in a timely manner how they are doing, what is working, and what is not working.

Feedback can come from many different sources: managers and supervisors, measurement systems, peers, and customers, just to name a few. Using multiple sources of feedback, which is sometimes called 360-degree assessment or multirater appraisal, is done in a variety of ways, but most methods are computerized and the raters are anonymous. Whether you need or want to use multirater appraisal depends on what you want to measure. For example, if you want to measure customer satisfaction, the best way to get the information is to ask the customer directly. (If customer survey tools are not available, or they are too expensive to develop, you may have to rely on other feedback sources, such as the number of complaints received.)

However feedback occurs, certain factors ensure its effectiveness:

SPECIFICITY  Feedback works best when it relates to a specific goal, such as those established in elements and standards. Basing feedback on the employee's performance against his or her elements and standards is key to providing tangible, objective, and powerful feedback. Telling employees that they are doing well because they exceeded their goal by 10 percent is more effective than simply saying "you're doing a good job."

TIMELINESS  Employees should receive information about how they are doing in as timely a fashion as possible. If they need to improve their performance, the sooner they find out about it, the sooner they can correct the problem. If employees have reached or exceeded a goal, the sooner they receive positive feedback, the more rewarding it is to them.

MANNER  Give feedback in a manner that will best help improve performance. Since people respond better to information presented in a positive way, express feedback in a positive manner. This is not to say that information should be sugar-coated. Present accurate, factual, and complete feedback; it is more effective when it reinforces what the employee did right and then identifies what the employee needs to do in the future. Constant criticism eventually falls on deaf ears.

NATURALLY OCCURRING FEEDBACK  Some kinds of feedback occur naturally while other kinds require careful planning and management.  Naturally occurring feedback can be classified into two categories. The first type is self-evident feedback—information that employees can see for themselves as they do their work. For instance, a team of materials handlers who are given the assignment of moving ten stacks of supplies from one side of the warehouse to the other by the end of the day will know that if only one of ten stacks is moved by noon, it is not likely to complete the assignment on time. This information is self-evident and is obtained by the employees making their own comparisons against a specific goal.

Another kind of self-evident feedback can be gained by having a broader scope of work. The broader the employee's scope of work, the better the employee can determine the quality of the finished product. For example, a writer/editor assigned to write a portion of an article may feel satisfied with the section he wrote. But the same writer/editor , if assigned responsibility for the entire article, would see that his independently written section had no relation to the rest of the article and needed revision.

The second category of naturally occurring feedback is carefully planned feedback characterized by automatic, frequent delivery through a measurement system. It is possible to design feedback into a work process or a measurement system so that employees receive it automatically. For example, feedback loops designed into many work processes provide performance measures daily, such as a production or printing process (i.e., number of copies printed per day as determined by machine count). Also, total quality and reengineering programs use extensive work process measurement methods. Employees measure for themselves how they and their team are doing.

Designing effective feedback into a performance management program will improve individual and team performance and will make your organization more effective. With effective feedback processes, employees can see their progress and that motivates them to reach their performance goals successfully.

# example feedback sources

*RETIREMENT BENEFITS SPECIALIST*

| ELEMENT | GENERAL MEASURES | SPECIFIC MEASURES | STANDARDS* | | | FEEDBACK SOURCE FOR MONITORING |
|---|---|---|---|---|---|---|
| | | | MINIMALLY SUCCESSFUL | FULLY SUCCESSFUL | EXCEEDS FULLY SUCCESSFUL | |
| Completed *claims* ▌Critical Element ▌50 priority points | Quality | The accuracy of annuity amounts. The completeness of the paperwork | 82-87% of annuity amounts are accurate and of claims are complete | 88-93% of annuity amounts are accurate and of claims are complete | 94-97 % of annuity amounts are accurate and of claims are complete | Data from automated system |
| | Quantity | The number of claims processed per week | 10-12 claims processed per week | 13-16 claims processed per week | 17-20 claims processed per week | Data from automated system |
| | Timeliness | The average number of days it takes to process a claim | An average of 101-110 days to complete claim | An average of 90-100 days to complete claim | An average of 75-90 days to complete claim | Data from automated system |
| *Guidance* and *technical assistance* to other specialists ▌Critical Element ▌35 priority points | Quality | The accuracy of the information, as determined by supervisor | Usually accurate | Usually accurate | Almost always accurate | Random supervisor observation and 360-degree tool |
| | | The perceptions of other specialists that the incumbent is willing to assist and that feedback is helpful | 50-59% of specialists agree that incumbent is routinely willing to assist and that feedback is helpful | 60-80% of specialists agree that incumbent is routinely willing to assist and that feedback is helpful | 81-89% of specialists agree that incumbent is routinely willing to assist and that feedback is helpful | |
| | Timeliness | The number of hours it takes for the incumbent to respond to other specialists' requests for assistance | Usually responds within 9-12 working hours from receipt of request | Usually responds within 4-8 working hours from receipt of request | Usually responds within 2-3 working hours from receipt of request | 360-degree tool |
| **Claims Division:** Division *claims* processed in less time and with lower error rates ▌Non-Critical Element ▌15 priority points | Quality | The accuracy rate of annuity amounts for the whole Division | N/A** | 88-93% annuity amounts are accurate | 94-97 % annuity amounts are accurate | Data from automated system |
| | Quantity | The number of claims the Division processes per week | | 220-230 claims processed by Division per week | 231-244 claims processed by Division per week | Data from automated system |
| | Timeliness | The average number of days it takes to process a claim | | An average of 90-100 days to complete claim | An average of 75-90 days to complete claim | Data from automated system |

| ELEMENT | GENERAL MEASURES | SPECIFIC MEASURES | STANDARDS* | | | FEEDBACK SOURCE FOR MONITORING |
| --- | --- | --- | --- | --- | --- | --- |
| | | | MINIMALLY SUCCESSFUL | FULLY SUCCESSFUL | EXCEEDS FULLY SUCCESSFUL | |
| Suggestion(s) for improving the process (for special individual recognition)<br><br>丨 Additional Performance Element<br><br>丨 0 priority points | Quality | The supervisor's and reviewers' judgment that the suggestion(s) improve(s) efficiency, productivity, flexibility, and/or usability | N/A** | Management and Division members determine that the suggestion(s) is/are worth adopting | Management and Division members determine that the suggestion(s) is/are worth adopting | Supervisor and Branch members' judgment |
| | Quantity | The number of suggestions made | | Incumbent provides 1-2 adopted suggestions per year | Incumbent provides 3-5 adopted suggestions per year. | Supervisor tracks |
| | Cost Effectiveness | The amount of money saved by adopting the suggestion. | | The incumbent's suggestions saved up to 10% of costs | The incumbent's suggestions saved up to 10-25% of costs | Data from automated system |
| **Claims Division:** Increased number of employees who can process claims<br><br>丨 Additional Performance Element<br><br>丨 0 priority points | Quantity | The number of employees who can do claims | N/A** | 35-50% of Division employees can process claims | 51-75% of Division employees can process claims | Supervisor observation |
| | Quality | The accuracy rate of annuities processed | | 88-93% of annuity amounts are accurate | 94-97% of annuity amounts are accurate | Data from automated system |

*To meet the performance level of the standards described for each element, each listed part of the standard must be present or occur.
**The Division decided that there was no benefit to establishing a *Minimally Successful* standard for a non-critical or an additional performance element.

## EXERCISE ON DEFINING FEEDBACK SOURCES

Now that you have developed elements, measures, and standards in previous exercises, what are the best sources of feedback for those elements? How often is it feasible to receive feedback? Who needs to see the feedback? Write down those sources of feedback under the column labeled "Feedback Source" on the foldout form on the back cover.

**FOLD OVER INSIDE BACK COVER FLAP AS SHOWN TO FILL OUT CHART**

Once you have developed a performance plan using the previous seven steps, checking your work is always a good idea. Use the checklist below to ensure that the elements and standards you developed to include in the performance plan are effective and meet regulatory requirements:

- Are the critical elements truly critical? Does failure on the critical element mean that the employee's overall performance is unacceptable?

- Is the range of acceptable performance clear? Are the performance expectations quantifiable, observable, and/or verifiable?

- Are the standards attainable? Are expectations reasonable?

- Are the standards challenging? Does the work unit or employee need to exert a reasonable amount of effort to reach the fully successful performance level?

- Are the standards fair? Are they comparable to expectations for other employees in similar positions? Do they allow for some margin of error?

- Are the standards applicable? Can the appraiser(s) use the standards to appraise performance? Can the appraiser(s) manage the data collected through the measurement process?

- Will work units and employees understand what is required?

- Are the elements and standards flexible? Can they be adapted readily to changes in resources or objectives?

- If your program permits appraising elements at levels above the *Fully Successful* or equivalent level, is the *Fully Successful* or equivalent standard surpassable? Is it possible for a work unit's or an employee's performance to exceed it?

# Guiding Principles for Performance Measurement

The principles listed below contain some valuable lessons learned about measuring performance.

### VIEW PERFORMANCE MEASUREMENT AS A VALUABLE TOOL, NOT AS AN EVIL

People view measurement systems from at least two different perspectives. When used constructively, they see a measurement system as a helpful feedback tool that provides information to managers and employees about how well they are doing in reaching their goals and where they might have room for improvement. It also provides information on which to base awards and recognition. When used poorly, however, people see a measurement system as a punishing club with which to hit people over the head if the numbers or results are bad. Managers and employees must trust that the measurement system is beneficial to them and the organization; otherwise, the temptation to game the numbers to avoid discipline will overwhelm them.

### ACCEPTANCE OF THE PERFORMANCE MEASUREMENT PROCESS IS ESSENTIAL TO ITS SUCCESS

Involving employees in the development of the elements and standards included in the performance plan is an excellent way to clarify expectations and measurement terminology. Active employee participation in creating valid measures that accurately reflect performance decreases the possibility that employees may feel manipulated through the measurement system.

### MEASURE WHAT IS IMPORTANT—NOT WHAT IS EASY TO MEASURE

It is easy to count the number of days since a project began, but if that is all that you measure, is that enough information to assess performance? No, probably not. Or if, for example, a customer service team only measures the number of calls that come into the team (the easy measure) and does not attempt to measure customer satisfaction with its service (the more difficult measure), the team does not have complete information about its performance and has no idea how well it is serving its customers. In addition, because what gets measured gets done, the team will probably focus on how it can increase the number of calls it receives and ignore the quality of service it provides.

As a result, organizations need to anticipate the behavioral and unintended consequences of measuring performance. As an example, recently a medical laboratory came under fire because of the errors it made in certain of its cancer tests. A high number of cancer tests that the laboratory had approved as negative turned out to be wrong—cancer had actually been evident. An investigation found that the laboratory had been measuring and rewarding its employees on the number of slides they reviewed daily, not on the accuracy of the reviews. Knowing that the more slides they reviewed, the more recognition they received, employees were quickly moving from slide to slide to slide without accurately reading them. As a result, the lab's errors in measuring what was important allowed cancer to go untreated and people who could have been saved through early detection and treatment lost their lives.

DEVELOP EMPLOYEE PERFORMANCE PLANS THAT ARE FLEXIBLE ENOUGH TO ALLOW FOR CHANGES IN PROGRAM GOALS TO KEEP THE PROCESS CREDIBLE  Do not design performance plans that are set in concrete; build in flexibility so you can adjust them as program goals and work assignments change. Even though employees must work at least a minimum period of time on elements and standards before they receive performance ratings, the agency minimum appraisal period usually provides enough time during the appraisal period for changes in elements and standards. (Minimum appraisal periods usually range from 30-120 days, depending on the agency. Check with your agency to find out the minimum appraisal period that applies to you.)

RELY ON MULTIPLE MEASURES  Don't rely on a single measure. Remember the story of the three blind men who went for a walk and came across an elephant? One felt the animal's trunk and claimed that the elephant was like a large snake. Another explored the elephant's leg and claimed that the elephant was like a big tree trunk. The third blind man touched the elephant's side and said that the elephant was like a tall, wide wall. All three of them were right, but all of them were wrong. Each one was relying on only one measure from one perspective. If the measures had been used together, the three men would have had a more accurate picture of the elephant.

EMPLOYEES SHOULD PERCEIVE THAT PERFORMANCE MEASUREMENT IS IMPORTANT In many organizations, employees have been exposed to a variety of management fads that seem to appear and then fade away as the next fad takes its place. Employees need to know that management is serious and committed to measuring and improving performance.

MANAGEMENT SHOULD DEMONSTRATE THAT PERFORMANCE IS CRITICAL TO ORGANIZATIONAL AND INDIVIDUAL SUCCESS  Closely related to the previous principle, this principle observes that not only should employees perceive that performance measurement is important, but also management must demonstrate that performance matters. When management tolerated poor performance in the past and employees see that the new measurement system has not changed the situation (in other words, Joe or Mary still comes to work and reads the paper for most of the day), employees know that performance is not important, despite the new system.

LEARNING AIDS

# Performance Measurement Quiz

Circle the correct answer(s).

1. Circle the accomplishments listed below:

   a. A completed, accurate report
   b. Types reports and correspondence
   c. Teamwork
   d. Guidance and technical assistance
   e. Satisfied customers
   f. Answers phones

2. Non-critical elements have to be weighted less than critical elements.

   a. True
   b. False

3. Standards should be written in terms of specific measures.

   a. True
   b. False

4. Which of the following is/are NOT regulatory requirements for critical elements?

   a. Each employee must have a minimum of one critical element
   b. Critical elements must measure individual performance
   c. Critical elements generally can be used to measure team-level performance
   d. Critical elements must have an established standard at least at a *Fully Successful* level
   e. Critical elements must be given greater weight than non-critical elements in deriving a summary level rating

5. Which of the following statement(s) is/are true about feedback?

   a. Peers can be included as sources of input for appraisals
   b. Feedback should be specific
   c. Whether to use 360-degree feedback depends on what you're measuring
   d. Feedback should be timely
   e. Feedback should be given in a manner that will best help improve performance
   f. All of the above are true

# chapter 4

6. Performance plans must be built from the employee's position description.
   a. True
   b. False

7. You can't measure results at the individual level.
   a. True
   b. False

8. The four general measures for measuring employee and work unit performance are cost-effectiveness, quantity, timeliness, and:
   a. Flexibility
   b. Quality
   c. Agency strategy
   d. Teamwork

9. Absolute standards can never be used.
   a. True
   b. False

10. A *Fully Successful* standard is a retention standard when (circle one or more):
   a. The standard is used in a Pass/Fail program with critical elements appraised at only two levels
   b. When there is no *Minimally Successful* level available in the appraisal program
   c. None of the above.

11. Measurement should be used for performance improvement.
   a. True
   b. False

ANSWERS ON PAGE 88

# Quick Reference: The Eight-Step Process

**STEP 1**      **LOOK AT THE OVERALL PICTURE**

Review organizational goals and objectives and performance measures already available. Determine which goals and measures the employee's work unit can affect.

**STEP 2**      **DETERMINE WORK UNIT ACCOMPLISHMENTS USING ANY OR ALL OF THE FOLLOWING METHODS:**

    *METHOD A*      *A GOAL CASCADING METHOD*

Cascade the agency's goals to the work unit level. Determine the work unit's accomplishment(s) that directly affect the organization's goals.

    *METHOD B*      *A CUSTOMER-FOCUSED METHOD*

Determine the product(s) or service(s) that the work unit provides to its customers.

    *METHOD C*      *A WORK FLOW CHARTING METHOD*

Develop a work flow chart for the work unit, establishing key steps(s) in the work process.

**STEP 3**      **DETERMINE INDIVIDUAL ACCOMPLISHMENTS THAT SUPPORT WORK UNIT GOALS**

Elements that address individual performance can be identified using a role-results matrix. List the work unit accomplishments across the top of the matrix. List each member of the work unit or each job position down the left side of the matrix. In each cell, list the accomplishment (i.e., performance element) that the member must produce or perform to support the work unit accomplishment. All performance elements should be either quantifiable or verifiable.

**STEP 4**      **CONVERT EXPECTED ACCOMPLISHMENTS INTO PERFORMANCE ELEMENTS, INDICATING TYPE AND PRIORITY**

All employees must have at least one critical element. Critical elements must address individual performance only. Work unit performance can be addressed through non-critical or additional elements. In appraisal programs with only two summary levels, work unit performance can be addressed only through additional performance elements.

**STEP 5**    **DETERMINE WORK UNIT AND INDIVIDUAL MEASURES**

For each element, determine which general measure(s) (i.e., quantity, quality, timeliness, or cost-effectiveness) are important. Determine how to measure the quantity, quality, timeliness, and/or cost-effectiveness for the element. If an accomplishment can be measured with numbers, determine the unit of measurement to be used. If performance can only be described (i.e., observed and verified), clarify who would appraise the work and what factors they would look for.

**STEP 6**    **DEVELOP WORK UNIT AND INDIVIDUAL STANDARDS**

A *Fully Successful* or equivalent standard must be established for each critical element. If the measure for the element is numeric, determine the range of numbers that would represent *Fully Successful* performance. For critical elements appraised at two levels, the *Fully Successful* standard identifies the level of performance below which performance is *Unacceptable.* For critical elements appraised at more than two levels, establish a range of performance above which special recognition may be warranted and below which a performance problem exists.

If the measure for the element is descriptive, determine what the appraiser would see or report that would verify that performance is *Fully Successful.* For critical elements appraised at two levels, describe performance for that element below which is *Unacceptable* performance. For elements appraised at more than two levels, and for elements for which stretch goals are desired, determine what exceeding expectations would look like. Describe what the appraiser would see happening when expectations are exceeded.

**STEP 7**    **DETERMINE HOW TO MONITOR PERFORMANCE**

Determine what data to collect for each performance element, which source the data should come from, and whether to collect all the data or just a sample. Determine when to collect the data, who should collect it, and who should receive it. Review existing reports for possible use as feedback reports. Create feedback tables or graphs where appropriate or necessary. Try to design feedback processes that give employees feedback automatically.

**STEP 8**    ***CHECK THE PERFORMANCE PLAN USING THE FOLLOWING GUIDELINES:***

| Are the critical elements truly critical? Does failure on the critical element mean that the employee's overall performance is unacceptable?

| Is the range of acceptable performance clear? Are the performance expectations quantifiable, observable, and/or verifiable?

| Are the standards attainable? Are expectations reasonable?

| Are the standards challenging? Does the work unit or employee need to exert a reasonable amount of effort to reach a fully successful performance level?

| Are the standards fair? Are they comparable to expectations for other employees in similar positions? Do they allow for some margin of error?

| Are the standards applicable? Can the appraiser(s) use the standards to appraise performance? Can the appraiser(s) manage the data collected through the measurement process?

| Will work units and employees understand what is required?

| Are the elements and standards flexible? Can they be adapted readily to changes in resources or objectives?

| If your program permits appraising elements at levels above the *Fully Successful* or equivalent level, is the *Fully Successful* or equivalent standard surpassable? Is it possible for a work unit's or an employee's performance to exceed it?

# Five-Level Appraisal–Examples

**THE FOLLOWING EXAMPLES OF ELEMENTS AND STANDARDS WERE WRITTEN SPECIFICALLY FOR APPRAISAL PROGRAMS THAT APPRAISE PERFORMANCE ON ELEMENTS AT FIVE LEVELS.**

*HUMAN RESOURCES ASSISTANT*

| ELEMENT | STANDARDS* |
|---------|-----------|
| **CUSTOMER SATISFACTION** | *FULLY SUCCESSFUL STANDARD*<br>(To meet this standard, the employee must meet all of the following requirements).<br><br>As determined by the supervisor through direct observation and/or discussions with several customers and/or peers:<br><br>│ Usually communicates clearly, courteously, and effectively with customers<br><br>│ Routinely responds to each customer request with the most accurate and complete information available. If the information to a telephone call can not be provided immediately upon request, usually provides an answer within 3 working days of receipt of call. Email responses are usually answered within 5 working days. Formal written correspondence is produced within agencywide standards (usually 10 working days)<br><br>│ Generally mails requested information within 3 working days of receipt of request<br><br>│ Whenever possible, elicits customer feedback to improve service<br><br>│ If the employee cannot answer a customer's question completely, he/she generally provides name and phone number for the proper contact. If the question requires additional research, keeps the customer apprised of progress<br><br>│ If requested material is temporarily unavailable to mail to customers, usually notifies the customers when they may expect to receive it<br><br>*OUTSTANDING STANDARD*<br>Exceeds the *Fully Successful* standard plus two of the following occur:<br><br>│ Receives praise and/or written commendations from customers<br><br>│ On own initiative, assumes and accomplishes a significant amount of work beyond the normal load of assigned duties to achieve customer satisfaction<br><br>│ Proactively communicates with customers to establish good working relationship and assess customer needs<br><br>│ Consistently demonstrates in-depth knowledge of customer programs<br><br>*MINIMALLLY SUCCESSFUL STANDARD*<br>The employee meets the first two requirements listed for *Fully Successful* and of the four remaining requirements, meets all but number(s) <u>4 & 6</u> . |

*Note: We have purposely listed the Minimally Successful standard last to emphasize performance that is Fully Successful and higher more than performance that is less than Fully Successful.*

*The standards include measures that can be tracked without using a customer survey. *Exceeds Fully Successful* falls between the performance described for *Fully Successful* and that described for *Outstanding*. *Unacceptable* performance falls below the minimum of *Minimally Successful*.

*HUMAN RESOURCES SPECIALIST*

| ELEMENT | STANDARDS* |
|---|---|
| **HR POLICY PRODUCTS** (e.g., written guidance, reports, overviews, workshops, formal presentations) | *FULLY SUCCESSFUL* STANDARD (To meet this standard, the employee must meet all of the following requirements.) **QUALITY** <br><br> Written products generally follow plain English principles, including logical organization, descriptive section headings, simple terms, and good use of tables, lists, graphics, and white space <br><br> Assigned presentations and workshops are generally well-organized with a logical flow, a use of simple terms, and graphics that illustrate concepts to help audience understanding. The overall audience rating of any presentation given is at least acceptable <br><br> Products usually reflect sound analytical thinking and present recommendations consistent with sound HR principles and supportive of Administration initiatives <br><br> **QUANTITY** <br><br> Produces (or does significant work for) <br> a) at least one major product (e.g., a workshop; a complex paper or report, often over 10 pages long) <br> b) at least three intermediate-in-scope products (e.g., topic papers 3-10 pages long) <br> c) at least five minor products (e.g., articles or 1-2 page papers) <br> d) a combination of these <br>   (To meet the definition of "produces," the report or paper at least must be cleared by the Division Chief.) <br><br> **TIMELINESS** <br><br> Draft written products are usually completed and submitted for review by the date agreed to at initial assignment. Revisions are usually done and returned within the agreed-upon time frame <br><br> *OUTSTANDING* STANDARD <br> Produces more than two major products, more than five intermediate-in-scope products, more than eight minor products, OR a combination of these <br><br> Exceeds the quality and timeliness criteria <br><br> Plus meets at least three of the following: <br> a) On own initiative, proposes the subject of the product <br> b) Completes extensive research to complete the product <br> c) Develops applicable, understandable models and examples <br> d) Synthesizes complex issues and condenses and explains them so that they are understandable to a general audience <br> e) Product content provides leadership in the program, fits the HR policy into the big picture of management, links HR policy to organizational goals, and/or highlights the links of HR policy with other management functions <br> f) Develops original understandable graphics that illustrate the concept being presented <br><br> *MINIMALLY SUCCESSFUL* STANDARD <br> The employee accomplishes the work described at the *Fully Successful* level except that intermediate and minor products of a routine nature are produced with moderate but not excessive rework. |

*Note: We have purposely listed the Minimally Successful standard last to emphasize performance that is Fully Successful and higher more than performance that is less than Fully Successful.*

*Exceeds Fully Successful falls between the performance described for *Fully Successful* and that described for *Outstanding*. Unacceptable falls below *Minimally Successful*.

*MEDICAL RECORDS TECHNICIAN*

| ELEMENT | STANDARDS* |
|---|---|
| **MEDICAL RECORDS** that include accurately filed documentation | **FULLY SUCCESSFUL STANDARD**<br>(To meet this standard, the employee must meet all of the following requirements.) As determined by the supervisor and from doctor/clinic feedback:<br><br>*QUALITY*<br><br>❙ Paperwork is usually filed according to hospital documentation regulations, with only a few errors or complaints<br><br>❙ With few exceptions, paperwork is date stamped the same day it arrives in the Medical Records Section<br><br>❙ The employee can usually locate records, whether they are in their filing shelves or checked out to doctors/clinics<br><br>❙ With few exceptions, medical records requested by a doctor/clinic/emergency room contain the paperwork received by the Medical Records Section within the last 3 working days, with contents usually filed accurately<br><br>*QUANTITY*<br><br>❙ The backlog of paperwork to be filed usually does not exceed the amount received within the last 3 working days<br><br>*TIMELINESS*<br><br>❙ Medical records are usually supplied to requestors by the time requested. In emergency situations, medical records are supplied consistently within an hour of request<br><br>**OUTSTANDING STANDARD**<br>The employee exceeds the *Fully Successful* standard plus meets all of the following:<br><br>❙ On own initiative, systematically reviews assigned files to ensure accuracy of paperwork placement in the file<br><br>❙ Very few records are more than three inches thick (i.e., overly thick files have been split into additional volumes)<br><br>❙ Voluntarily conducts systematic searches for missing paperwork or records, including verifying checkout cards<br><br>❙ At least one of the employee's suggestions for improvements in the filing process or to records management is adopted<br><br>❙ Most medical record jackets are in good condition (i.e., torn or worn jackets have been replaced, as supplies allow)<br><br>*MINIMALLY SUCCESSFUL STANDARD*<br>To meet this standard, the employee completes the requirements of the *Fully Successful* standard except that the backlog often exceeds 3 days but usually does not exceed 4 days and the _third_ quality requirement is not met. |

*Note: We have purposely listed the Minimally Successful standard last to emphasize performance that is Fully Successful and higher more than performance that is less than Fully Successful.*

*Exceeds Fully Successful falls between the performance described for Fully Successful and that described for Outstanding. Unacceptable falls below Minimally Successful.*

*HUMAN RESOURCES SPECIALIST (EMPLOYEE RELATIONS)*

| ELEMENT | STANDARDS* |
|---|---|
| **TECHNICAL INFORMATION, ADVICE, AND ASSISTANCE** | *FULLY SUCCESSFUL* STANDARD<br><br>▎ Provides timely and reliable technical advice and assistance to agency and other officials on employee relations and appellate matters. Advice is based on good knowledge and proper application of regulation, precedent cases, and relationships among human resources programs. Discusses advantages, disadvantages, and feasible options in connection with issues and problems presented. Coordinates with other agency offices, as appropriate. Brings unique or potentially difficult issues and problems to the attention of the supervisor with options and recommendations for further action<br>▎ Gains useful feedback from agencies and other organizations within the agency on the impact of policies and processes under the employee relations program. Provides suggestions on how best to use information and insights to improve employee relations programs and procedures<br>▎ Thoroughly reviews and provides timely comments on materials presented for review by other offices. Comments take into account applicable regulations, case law, and policy objectives in the areas of employee relations and appellate policies. Training and briefings provided to employees are well conceived, effectively presented, and well received<br><br>*OUTSTANDING STANDARD:*<br>▎ Is uncommonly effective in dealing with officials who present difficult issues and problems for resolution. Options and recommended solutions are creative, pertinent, and demonstrate an in-depth understanding of the issues. Where appropriate, recites successful practices and programs in other agencies. Displays deep knowledge of HRM policies, precedent cases, agency needs, and the likely impact on management and employees of solution proposed<br>▎ Based on knowledge and insights, is able to propose significant changes to policies and procedures which hold the potential for improvement<br>▎ In reviewing the products of other organizations, is able to point out major issues or problems not otherwise foreseen or to make suggestions for significant improvement as warranted<br>▎ Is able to cause major changes in policies to be considered, where appropriate, through the persuasiveness and thoroughness of written comments and/or informal meetings<br>▎ Review and commentary is timely, even in the event of competing priorities and large workload<br><br>*MINIMALLY SUCCESSFUL STANDARD:*<br><br>▎ Answers to questions about employee relations policies are usually accurate and provided in a timely manner<br>▎ Regularly gains useful feedback from organizations on agency policies and programs in employee relations. Occasionally surfaces feedback in a manner that is useful to management<br>▎ As requested, furnishes comments to other offices on proposed policy materials, training courses, and legislation. Comments point out technical inaccuracies or inconsistency with established policy |

*Note: We have purposely listed the Minimally Successful standard last to emphasize performance that is Fully Successful and higher more than performance that is less than Fully Successful.*

*Exceeds Fully Successful falls between the performance described for Fully Successful and that described for Outstanding. Unacceptable falls below Minimally Successful. This example does not include a Minimally Successful standard.*

ATTORNEY ADVISOR

| ELEMENT | STANDARDS* |
|---|---|
| **WRITTEN MATERIALS** (e.g., legal memoranda, briefs, and pleadings) | *FULLY SUCCESSFUL STANDARD* (must meet all of the following) <br><br> **QUALITY** <br><br> As determined by the supervisor, written materials <br> • Are generally considered to be of average professional quality <br> • Are infrequently returned for substantial revision <br> • Usually fully analyze relevant legal and policy issues <br> • Usually reflect thorough investigation of factual and legal resources <br> • Usually do not contain significant extraneous or inappropriate material <br><br> **QUANTITY** <br><br> • In most instances, written materials are developed as needed <br><br> **TIMELINESS** <br><br> • Written materials are generally completed and presented in accordance with established deadlines or time frames <br><br> *OUTSTANDING STANDARD* (must meet all of the following) <br><br> Written materials: <br> • Are routinely considered to be of highest professional quality <br> • Are rarely returned for substantial revision <br> • Consistently fully analyze relevant legal and policy issues <br> • Reflect thorough investigation of factual and legal resources <br> • Do not contain significant extraneous or inappropriate material <br> • Are completed before established deadlines or time frames <br> • Are always completed as needed |

*Exceeds Fully Successful falls between the performance described for *Fully Successful* and that described for *Outstanding*. Unacceptable falls below *Minimally Successful*. This example does not include a *Minimally Successful* standard.

NOTE: We have purposely left out a Minimally Successful standard in this example to emphasize performance that is Fully Successful and higher. In the event that an employee's performance fell below the Fully Successful level, a Minimally Successful standard would be established and communicated.

# Three-Level Appraisal–Examples

**THE FOLLOWING EXAMPLES OF ELEMENTS AND STANDARDS WERE WRITTEN SPECIFICALLY FOR APPRAISAL PROGRAMS THAT APPRAISE PERFORMANCE ON ELEMENTS AT THREE LEVELS.**

TEAM LEADER, PACKAGING PRODUCTION TEAM

| ELEMENT | FULLY SUCCESSFUL STANDARD* <br> (To meet the *Fully Successful* standard for an element, all of the bullets listed for the element must be met.) |
|---|---|
| Quality products | ▪ Usually 90% to 95% of pallets have no defects <br> ▪ With few exceptions, no more than 1.5 to 2 hours of down time per week <br> ▪ Normally, the packaging production schedule is met 5 out of 7 days <br> ▪ Normally, the shipment schedule is met 5 out of 7 days |
| Safe work environment | ▪ Safety problems are corrected or improvements usually are made by agreed-on date <br> ▪ Routinely holds one safety audit per week <br> ▪ Very rarely has any lost time hours |
| Effective leadership | ▪ Team goals are met 60-80% of the time <br> ▪ Manager judges that the team leader periodically initiates ways to reduce costs <br> ▪ Manager judges that decisions are well thought out and support organizational goals. |
| Productive subordinates | Manager is generally satisfied that: <br> ▪ Training requirements of the team are met <br> ▪ Discipline is provided fairly and consistently <br> ▪ Most team members understand the department's goals and how their performance affects these goals <br> ▪ Team members understand how they're performing against their goals <br> ▪ Team members receive rewards for good performance |

*To achieve the *Outstanding* level, the employee must consistently exceed a majority of the bullets listed for the *Fully Successful* standard. *Unacceptable* performance occurs when the employee fails to meet one or more of the bullets listed for *Fully Successful* performance.

PROGRAM ANALYST

| ELEMENT: ORAL PRESENTATIONS |
| --- |
| STANDARDS* (To meet a standard, all of the statements listed for the standard must be met.) |

### OUTSTANDING STANDARD

When attendee evaluations are available:

| Sixty to eighty-four percent of attendees rated the employee's presentation good or very good.

When attendee evaluations are not available, the supervisor determines that the employee:

| Presents information in a clear, concise, and well-organized manner

| Responds well to questions, including unanticipated ones

| Creates a favorable impression for effective communication by seeking the views of others and respecting different points of view

| Asks probing questions to ensure that everyone understands the matters discussed

| Clearly distinguishes between fact and opinion and avoids disclosing sensitive or tentative information prematurely

| Listens well, responds appropriately and articulately, and remains calm in adverse situations

| Knows when and how to use visual aids, speaks authoritatively on subject matter , and displays ability to respond directly to questions raised

| Encourages active participation by others

| Senses audience's receptivity to presentation and adjusts accordingly

| Shows thorough knowledge of issues and their relationship to broader issues

| Presents technical information clearly and persuasively, demonstrating the importance and relevancy of planning.

### FULLY SUCCESSFUL STANDARD

When attendee evaluations are available:

| More than 60-84% of attendees rated the employee's presentation good or very good

When attendee evaluations are not available, the supervisor determines that the employee:

| Usually presents information clearly, concisely, and in a well-organized manner

| Routinely shows respect for comments of participants

| Generally keeps discussion on track

| Usually elicits comments of others

| Generally weighs consequences of statements before speaking, clearly distinguishing between fact and opinion, and avoids disclosing sensitive or tentative information prematurely

| Usually listens well, responds to issues at hand, and minimizes extraneous information

| Usually answers most questions and invites additional questions to ensure understanding

*Unacceptable performance occurs when the employee fails to meet one or more of the bullets listed for  Fully Successful performance.

*GRAPHICS DESIGNER*

---

*ELEMENT: GRAPHIC DESIGNS*

---

*STANDARD*

*OUTSTANDING* STANDARD

In addition to meeting all criteria of the *Fully Successful* standard, the supervisor determines that the employee meets at least four of the following:

| Designs are often of such high quality that they generate spontaneous praise from clients

| The elegance of designs often enhances their purpose in unexpected ways

| Designs consistently reflect the highest professional standards and raise the standards for other agency designers

| The most complex design tasks are handled with little or no difficulty

| Suggestions are made that improve the agency's design processes

| Potential problems are anticipated, brought to the supervisor's attention as appropriate, and usually solved independently


*FULLY SUCCESSFUL* STANDARD

To meet this standard, all of the following must be met:

The supervisor determines that:

| The quality of information-material design is usually acceptable to the client and sufficient to achieve the purposes intended

| In most cases, designs are in accordance with the agency's graphic standards system and meet commonly accepted criteria for professional work

| Logical planning, due consideration of priorities, and efficient application of technical graphics skills usually result in creation of graphic designs in time to meet reasonable deadlines

| Generally nonwasteful work habits reflect a consideration of costs to the Government

| Instructions from supervisors are most often followed as given, major revisions are rarely necessary, and routine problems are usually resolved with a minimum of supervision

*TRAINING COORDINATOR*

| ELEMENT | FULLY SUCCESSFUL STANDARD * <br> (To meet the *Fully Successful* standard for an element, **all** of the bullets listed for the element must be met.) |
|---|---|
| CERTIFIED PROGRAMMERS | Most of the supervisors of certified programmers say that the trained programmer(s): <br><br> ▎ Could handle their assignments right away <br> ▎ Didn't bother coworkers and supervisor for covered objectives <br> ▎ Demonstrated certified skill/knowledge assessment was accurate <br><br> Recommended trainees generally complete the training within the following time frames: <br><br> ▎ Average of 18 to 25 working days to complete Phase I training <br> ▎ Average of 18 to 23 working days to complete Phase II training <br> ▎ Average of 10 to 15 working days to complete Phase III training <br><br> Most of the supervisors of the trained programmers say that the topics covered match what is needed on the job |
| TRAINING PLANS | ▎ Most internal customers agree that the training plan will meet their needs and commit dollars and trainee time <br> ▎ Supervisor is generally satisfied that the training plan contains standard components, has realistic time lines and objectives, is based on input from representative sample, and is consistent with agency long-range goals, objectives, and philosophy <br> ▎ The incumbent meets agreed-upon deadline for first approved draft |
| CROSS-TRAINED ANALYSTS | ▎ 60%-80% trainees meet learning objectives <br> ▎ Trainees' supervisors are generally satisfied with analysts' improvement in their ability to communicate with programmers and solve minor problems without a programmer |
| TRAINING FACILITY READY FOR TRAINING | The supervisor is generally satisfied that: <br><br> ▎ The training room is ready for training when needed <br> ▎ Materials are available <br> ▎ Speaker's needs have been determined and addressed |
| CUSTOMER SERVICE MANUAL | The supervisor is generally satisfied that the manual: <br><br> ▎ Covers most if not all job dimensions <br> ▎ Has most if not all standard components <br> ▎ The customer service supervisor says the document is useful |

*To achieve the *Outstanding* level, the employee must consistently exceed a majority of the bullets listed for the *Fully Successful* standard. *Unacceptable* performance occurs when the employee fails to meet one or more of the bullets listed for *Fully Successful* performance.

# Two-Level Appraisal–Examples

**THE FOLLOWING EXAMPLES OF ELEMENTS AND STANDARDS WERE WRITTEN SPECIFICALLY FOR APPRAISAL PROGRAMS THAT APPRAISE PERFORMANCE OF ELEMENTS AT ONLY TWO LEVELS.**

POLICY PROCESSING CLERK

| ELEMENT | FULLY SUCCESSFUL STANDARD<br>(To meet the *Fully Successful* standard for each element, **all** of the bullets listed for the element must be present or occur.) |
| --- | --- |
| COMPLETED AUDITS | • No more than 5 errors per month are found on audits<br><br>• For at least 10 weeks per year, no audits are more than 30 days old |
| QUOTES AND PROPOSALS | • No more than 5 quotes and proposals per month are found to be inaccurate at issuing<br><br>• No more than 5 quotes per month are processed in more than 5 days<br><br>• No more than 5 proposals per month are processed in more than 24 hours |
| SOLUTIONS | • No more than 2 times per quarter are incorrect results or procedures spotted by the supervisor or other team members<br><br>• No more than 2 times per quarter are problems corrected in more than 3 business days |
| FINISHED POLICIES | • No more than 5 errors per month are spotted by team members<br><br>• No more than 5 times per month when someone can't do the next step on a policy due to illegibility, incompleteness, or vagueness in the file<br><br>• No more than 3 times per month someone on the team gets a second call for the same issue/problem<br><br>• For at least 10 weeks per year, there are no changes more than 30 days old<br><br>• For at least 5 weeks per year, there is no new business more than 10 days old |
| ANSWERS TO QUESTIONS | • 60% of surveyed team members and a sample of people outside the team say:<br>— The technician stops what (s)he's doing and immediately tries to answer the question<br>— They don't find out later that the answer is wrong<br>— If the technician doesn't know the answer, (s)he either researches the solution or directs the person to the correct source |

RESEARCH CHEMIST

| ELEMENT | FULLY SUCCESSFUL STANDARD (To meet the *Fully Successful* standard for each element, **all** of the bullets listed for the element must be present or occur.) |
|---|---|
| ANALYTICAL RESULTS AND SPECIFICATIONS | The Research Manager is routinely satisfied that: <br><br> ❘ The method measures the appropriate variable <br><br> ❘ The results are relevant <br><br> ❘ The method is scientifically sound <br><br> ❘ There is a well-written protocol <br><br> ❘ The method is accurate, precise, reproducible, fast, and cost-effective <br><br> The customer is generally satisfied that: <br><br> ❘ They can understand and observe the results <br><br> ❘ The cost is within the budget <br><br> ❘ The information gives understandable answers to their questions |
| SOLUTIONS TO CUSTOMER PROBLEMS | The Research Manager is routinely satisfied that: <br><br> ❘ Reports and solutions address the question that was asked <br><br> ❘ The assumptions or hypotheses are based on scientific principles <br><br> ❘ The proposed solutions, suggestions, and/or recommendations are understandable <br><br> ❘ The recommendations were provided within the agreed-on time frame. <br><br> The customer is generally satisfied that: <br><br> ❘ The report and any answers to questions address the question that was asked <br><br> ❘ The proposed solutions, suggestions, and/or recommendations are understandable <br><br> ❘ The proposed recommendations were provided within the agreed-on time frame <br><br> ❘ The solutions work <br><br> ❘ The information gives understandable answers to their questions <br><br> ❘ They are able to implement the recommendations |

*ENGINEER*

| ELEMENT | FULLY SUCCESSFUL STANDARD<br>(To meet the *Fully Successful* standard for each element, **all**<br>of the bullets listed for the element must be present or occur .) |
|---|---|
| DESIGNS FOR CAPITAL IMPROVEMENTS AND OPERATIONS CHANGES | The supervisor is routinely satisfied that:<br><br>▎ The cost estimate is sufficiently itemized<br><br>▎ There is backup documentation for all cost estimates<br><br>▎ There is consistency across design documents<br><br>▎ The design looks like it will solve the problem or meet the need<br><br>▎ The design doesn't cause new problems while solving the original problem<br><br>In addition:<br><br>▎ There is no significant cost overrun due to inaccurate quantities<br><br>▎ The design is routinely completed by the agreed-on deadline |
| BUDGET REPORT | ▎ The budget report is generally submitted by the fifteenth day of the month<br><br>▎ The engineer is routinely able to answer questions about project financial status at any time |
| COMPLETED PROJECTS | The supervisor is routinely satisfied that:<br><br>▎ The project is constructed according to the design<br><br>▎ Unexpected conditions are successfully worked around<br><br>▎ Recommendations are made by agreed-on deadline<br><br>▎ The contract cost is within 5% of the estimate |

PROGRAM ANALYST (BUDGET)

| ELEMENT | FULLY SUCCESSFUL STANDARD<br>(To meet the *Fully Successful* standard for each element, **all** of the bullets listed for the element must be present or occur .) |
|---|---|
| BUSINESS DECISION RECOMMENDATIONS, INCLUDING BUDGET ANALYSIS AND COST INFORMATION/ANALYSIS | The supervisor is routinely satisfied that:<br><br>⏐ Cost impacts surrounding the decision have been identified and evaluated<br><br>⏐ The numbers are accurate and do not require second-guessing or rework<br><br>⏐ Reports/analysis logically state the issues and reach conclusions that are supported by the data and analysis<br><br>⏐ The analysis is useful and answers the question asked<br><br>⏐ The analysis/information was provided by the agreed-on deadline |
| FINANCIAL SYSTEMS IMPROVED | The supervisor as well as the users of the system are generally satisfied that:<br><br>⏐ The system change is within the scope of control<br><br>⏐ The change provides information in a more efficient, accurate, and useful manner than previously<br><br>⏐ The time required to implement the change meets the customer's needs and deadlines<br><br>⏐ The value of the improvements exceeds the cost of the implementation |
| BUDGET PROCESS EVALUATION AND ANALYSIS | The supervisor is routinely satisfied that:<br><br>⏐ The reports/analysis logically state the issues and reach conclusions that are supported by the data and analysis<br><br>⏐ The evaluations address all issues and cost impacts |

notes

_____

_____

_____

_____

_____

_____

_____

_____

_____

_____

_____

_____

## answers from page 19

**TRAINS EMPLOYEES—** *ACTIVITY,* **SUPERVISION—** *CATEGORY,* **A COMPLETED CASE—** *ACCOMPLISHMENT,* **PUBLIC RELATIONS—** *CATEGORY,*
**RECOMMENDATIONS—** *ACCOMPLISHMENT,* **CUSTOMER SERVICE—** *CATEGORY,* **HR POLICY INTERPRETATIONS—** *ACCOMPLISHMENT,*
**WRITES AGENCY POLICY—** *ACTIVITY,* **SOLUTIONS TO PROBLEMS—** *ACCOMPLISHMENT,* **DEVELOPS SOFTWARE PROGRAMS—** *ACTIVITY,*
**IDEAS AND INNOVATIONS—** *ACCOMPLISHMENT,* **FILES PAPERWORK—** *ACTIVITY,* **WRITES MEMOS—** *ACTIVITY,*
**COMPUTER SYSTEMS THAT WORK—** *ACCOMPLISHMENT,* **TEAMWORK—** *CATEGORY,* **A COMPLETED PROJECT—** *ACCOMPLISHMENT,*
**SATISFIED CUSTOMERS—** *ACCOMPLISHMENT,* **ANSWERS THE PHONE—** *ACTIVITY,* **ASSISTS TEAM MEMBERS—** *ACTIVITY*

## answers from pages 70-71

| | | |
|---|---|---|
| *1—* A D E | *5—* F | *9—* B |
| *2—* B | *6—* B | *10—* A B |
| *3—* A | *7—* B | *11—* A |
| *4—* C E | *8—* B | |

notes

notes

FOLD OVER INSIDE BACK COVER FLAP AS SHOWN TO FILL OUT CHART.
SEE PAGES 46, 51, 60, AND 66 FOR FURTHER INSTRUCTIONS

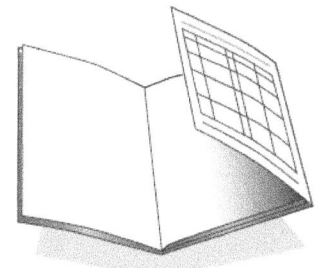

| PRIORITY POINTS | ELEMENT | TYPE | GENERAL MEASURE | SPECIFIC MEASURE | STANDARDS AND FEEDBACK |
|---|---|---|---|---|---|
|  |  |  |  |  |  |
|  |  |  |  |  |  |
|  |  |  |  |  |  |
|  |  |  |  |  |  |
|  |  |  |  |  |  |